People of the Townhouse

A History of the Native People of Tallassee, Alabama

By Debra Hughey

Wake Forest, NC

www.scuppernongpress.com

People of the Townhouse

©2012 Debra Hughey

First Printing

The Scuppernong Press
PO Box 1724
Wake Forest, NC 27588
www.scuppernongpress.com

Cover and book design by Frank B. Powell, III

All rights reserved. Printed in the United States of America.

No part of this book may be reproduced or transmitted in any form or by any means, electronic or mechanical, including photocopying, recording, or by any information and storage and retrieval system, without written permission from the editor and/or publisher.

International Standard Book Number ISBN 978-0-9845529-8-6

Library of Congress Control Number: 2012954525

Table of Contents

Introduction .... *iii*

Acknowledgments .... *v*

Chapter 1   Paleo People 1

Chapter 2   Archaic People 3

Chapter 3   Woodland People 7

Chapter 4   Mississippian People 11

Chapter 5   DeSoto and His Entourage 17

Chapter 6   The Muscogee, from where did
            they come? 19

Chapter 7   Home at Last 21

Chapter 8   Talisi 25

Chapter 9   Tuckabatchee 31

Chapter 10 Atasi Culture at Tuckabatchee 33

Chapter 11 Shawnee Newcomers & Tuckabatchee
            Plates 37

Chapter 12 Tallapoosa Culture at Tuckabatchee 39

Chapter 13 Late Tallapoosa Culture at Tuckabatchee .. 45

Chapter 14 Clan Social System 49

Chapter 15 Chiefs and Prophets 51

Chapter 16 Ball Play 53

Chapter 17 Talisi Royalty 57

Chapter 18 The Traders 61

Chapter 19 Visitors, Those Who Came
 and Those Who Stayed 65

Illustrations 68

Chapter 20 Cultural Breakdown 93

Chapter 21 The Shooting Star 95

Chapter 22 Tecumseh On the Tallapoosa 99

Chapter 23 The Speech 105

Chapter 24 Response and Final Words 107

Chapter 25 After the Shooting Star 111

Chapter 26 Rumbles of War 113

Chapter 27 The Siege 115

Chapter 28 Burnt Corn 119

Chapter 29 The Fort.. 123

Chapter 30 Autossee... 127

Chapter 31 Un-Holy Ground 133

Chapter 32 Calebee 135

Chapter 33 The Horseshoe 137

Chapter 34 After the Horseshoe 141

Chapter 35 The Treaty.. 145

Chapter 36 Back Home On the Tallapoosa 149

Chapter 37 Barent and Millie.................................153

Chapter 38 The Final Sunset 157

Epilogue.. 161

Bibliography... 163

Introduction

Today I have fulfilled a dream, a dream I have carried with me most of my life, the dream of writing a book about the indigenous people of my town, Tallassee, Alabama. I think this all began when I was three or four years old. My Daddy, the late Delma Taunton, instilled in me a great love of anything Native American. We — Daddy, Mama, and later my sister and I — would go, "down on the river" to hunt for Indian relics. Of course, we had permission to be on the "sacred" land, but back then, most landowners did not care, so we had the freedom to search the sites of Tuckabatchee and Talisi.

I remember sitting between rows of cotton, picking up dozens of little blue and black trade beads and later finding that perfect arrowhead. Oh, the thrill! I was hooked and have never lost that special feeling for my "Indians." I always wanted to be an archaeologist or an anthropologist, but never made that goal. When my husband, Randall Hughey, and I first began dating, he asked me what I liked to do. I knew that he fished on the Tallapoosa River, so I asked him if he could take me to some Indian sites. He did. We have spent many, many hours in wonderful and special places where we could feel the Spirit of the People who lived here first. Randall, over the years, for Christmas, my birthday or "just because," has given me more than two-hundred books on Native Americans.

So, now it is my turn. I would like to thank my late Daddy for instilling in me the love for my Indians, and my wonderful husband who has continued to encourage and inspire me to learn about the subject so dear to me.

I am not a scholar; my intention was to write a book which everyone can easily read, understand, and enjoy. Come with me now, to a different place in time … to a Tallassee of long ago.

Acknowledgments

Thanks for editing assistance from my writer friends,

W. C. Bryant

Charles Pollard

Larry Williamson

and

Special Thanks to my dear husband

Fred Randall Hughey

For many hours of typing and helpful suggestions

and

To my talented sister

Lessia Rothwein

for

The Cover Sketch

Chapter 1
Paleo People

They came.

Long before the town and place known as Tallassee, Alabama would be, they came. Thousands of years before the long bridge would span the magnificent river or the vast mills would dot the shoreline, they were here. Who were they and why did these people from the long distant past come to this particular place to live their lives?

Archaeologists call these people Paleo and they came originally from Siberia in northern Russia, crossing the frozen Bering Strait during the Ice Age, maybe 20,000 years ago. Thousands of years more would pass before small groups of nomadic bands would arrive here following the migration of the mastodon and giant bison. As the animals followed the winding rivers, searching for food supplies and for warmer climates, the people too would follow. Crossing Alaska they turned to the southeast into the current states of Kentucky and Tennessee where they gathered around the salt licks, essential for both animal and human life. Continuing to follow the magnificent river systems that meander through Alabama, the Paleo people entered the Tallapoosa River Valley. The Tallapoosa began as only a small creek trickling out of north Georgia, gaining strength from the many tributaries that would, in the far away future, bear the names of the people who would live on their banks. The Emuckfa, the Hillabee, the Kowaliga, and the Saugahatchee. The river continued to gain momentum, twisting and turning through the foothills of the Appalachian Mountains, cutting into the massive walls of granite, until finally spreading into the half mile-wide shoals which led to the roaring falls…the falls of the Tallapoosa.

Below the falls the landscape changed into a flat, fertile valley that begins the Gulf Coastal Plain, an ideal place to live then, just as it is now. The river provided fish and mussels. The hardwood forest furnished hickory nuts and acorns. Wild berries and natural fruits were abundant in spring.

The climate was moderate with cold-but-not-unbearable winters and warm, long summers. The small bands of family groups, must have found the area very pleasant. Archaeologist and Anthropologist Dr. John Cottier of Auburn University stated the Paleo People were in this area at least eight-thousand years ago. Six-thousand years before the birth of Jesus, these people welcomed the rising sun of each new day and must have wondered about the multitude of stars that sparkled in the night sky.

Although Paleo People had the knowledge and use of fire for warmth and crude cooking, their life was difficult. Their homes were natural habitation sites such as rock shelters or knolls near springs or small streams. They had no ability to store food, which meant each day they had to search for their sustenance. They did leave behind, evidence of being here, in the form of their lithic (stone) tools. The Paleo people produced a large variety of stone tools, including points of surprisingly good workmanship, as well as scrapers, knives, and choppers. They used spears and clubs and were undoubtedly efficient in the use of these weapons. Some of the artifacts have been found by many collectors in the Tallassee area. The Paleo way of life changed little over the next two or three-thousand years. Around five-thousand BC is considered a transition period. By four-thousand BC the Paleo people had evolved into what archaeologists refer to as the Archaic Period.

Chapter 2
Archaic People

During the Archaic period, the people still lived a hunter-gatherer life style. As time passed over the centuries, they gained more knowledge and learned to supplement their food supply in various ways. During this time period the Archaic People gathered mussels from the river shoals. They dug fire pits, lined the pit with river rocks, and broiled the mussels. They also heated stones over the fire and dropped them into stone, wooden, or possibly leather containers to cook their food. Stone bowl fragments have been found at many sites in the area and for a good reason. About four miles above the falls on the Tallapoosa County side of the river, near Coon Creek, is a natural bed of soapstone or steatite, of which the bowls were made.

* * * * * * *

One warm fall Sunday afternoon, after obtaining permission from the landowner, my husband and I, along with my sister, her husband and their daughter, made an excursion to the site. I had known about the soapstone site and had lived only a few miles away for most of my life, but had never had the opportunity to see it. My niece had previously seen the site and was excited to show it to me. It was amazing. Located on a hillside overlooking a small tributary of Coon Creek, was a large area of soapstone. Soapstone is a soft-but-tough material and was used not only for the manufacture of pots and bowls, but also for pipes, some quite elaborate. The intriguing fact about the quarry is that you can actually see where the pot or bowl was cut from the larger stone. In several cases, part of the bowl could still be seen.

There are several quarries of soapstone scattered throughout Chilton, Chambers and Tallapoosa Counties. This particular quarry was discovered by a State of Alabama geologist in the 1850s. In recent years the site has been investigated by archaeologist from the University of Alabama. It would be very interesting to know more about the site. I can imagine the Archaic miners meticulously carving their bowls from the larger stone, perhaps on a warm sunny afternoon. Like us they probably kept a close look out for the large rattlesnakes that frequent the hillside.

* * * * * * *

The Archaic people built temporary huts, and at some sites the remains of lithic workshops have been found. They learned the art of pecking, grinding and polishing and were able to produce stone beads, gorgets (a decorative piece worn about the neck), and axes, the previously mentioned pipes and the Atlatl or throwing stick.

The throwing stick was probably the main weapon used by the Archaic people and was used on into the woodland time period. The purpose of the "stick" was to add sort of an extension to the hunter's arm, allowing the spear to go further with greater velocity. It is quite a rare find for the artifact hunter to make, but many in the area have found the stone charm, which actually provided extra weight, allowing the leverage necessary for the throwing stick to function properly.

Using other natural materials available, such as bone, they made awls, needles, fishhooks, scrapers, pins, combs and projectile points. The Archaic people used plant fiber to make baskets and fish nets and also wood for their huts and canoes. During the later Archaic period, evidence shows that long-distance trade began to take place between the people of different regions outside the Tallapoosa River Valley.

The change that would make their lives easier was the invention or possibly the ability to create pottery. Pottery was first made on the Savannah River, near the current States of Georgia and South Carolina. This life-changing event occurred about three-thousand years ago.

The burial practices of the late Archaic people reflected changes ever so slowly, in lifestyles and also in the formation of cultures. A deceased person was buried near his hut in a circular grave, sometimes in the flexed or sitting position. Evidence of cremation has been found. Some burials include various personal items such as pipes and bowls.

They adapted well to the warmer climate and natural resources available in the Southland, and more particularly the area that would become in a few thousand years Tallassee, Alabama.

Most of the information about the Archaic People is general in nature for Alabama and the southeast, and comes from the book *Sun Circles and Human Hands, the Southeastern Indians-Art and Industry*, a wonderful book edited by Emma Lila Funderburk and Mary Douglas Foreman. I received this book as a gift from my husband back in 1983. The incredible price, including shipping, was $14.00!

Now, the following information is specific to Tallassee and comes from the awesome book I received in 2010 and which was many times more expensive than the previously mentioned book. *Tuckabatchee Archaeological Investigations at an Historic Creek Town, Elmore County, Alabama, 1984*, written by Vernon James Knight, Jr. This is a report of the archaeological research done at Tuckabatchee by Dr. Knight and the University of Alabama for the Industrial Development Board of the City of Tallassee, prior to the construction of the GKN-Aerospace facility. I will refer to both of these books many times.

In his research, Dr. Knight found evidence of habitation in the Tuckabatchee area, as did Dr. Cottier, that dates back to six to eight thousand B.C. The number of artifacts found was considerably small compared to later time periods' indicating the area was occupied by small groups. Flaked stone tools such as knives and scrapers were found, as well as pottery sherds. Projectile points better known as arrow heads were also found. The arrow heads were mostly made from quartz and occasionally coastal plain chert. Quartz-Quartzite as defined by Webster's Dictionary is a crystalline mineral, a form of silica, usually colorless and transparent. Another source describes quartz as variously colored semiprecious stones. A large quartzite vein or outcropping runs through

Central Alabama above the fall line. This is still visible on dirt roads in wooded areas. While most of the quartz in the Tallassee area is of the milky white variety, it is not uncommon to see stones totally transparent. Another type, more often found in Eastern Alabama is denser and appears in the colors of rosy pink, bluish gray and brown. Commonly known as Hollis Quartz, it is often confused with the harder flint, which is scarce in Central Alabama. Flint is native to Europe and the true flint found in Alabama likely arrived in Pensacola as ballast in ships. Quartz was used by the Indians to make chipped arrow points and tools. For the serious artifact hunter, it is always good to find an arrow of any type, but one made from chert is really special. Chert is a soft, fine-grained stone, also a form of silica found in limestone, that can be a variety of colors, brown, black, tan, even a pink or lavender. The chert point was made by percussion flaking and was a work of art. The Archaic artist used a deer antler or a stone tool to obtain the intricate flaking. Some people think the fingerprint of the Indian remains on the point. Of course, it's not his fingerprint, but the print of his ability. Some of the names of the points found at Tuckabatchee from the Archaic period include Big Sandy, Autauga, LeCrop and Decatur. The collections of local artifact hunters invariably contain arrow points made of quartz and chert. Strangely enough, the points and arrowheads from this period seem more meticulously made and are prettier than those made at later time periods.

We can only speculate how the Archaic people lived from the many things they left behind. The stone artifacts and tools that have withstood the test of thousands of years of time, is all that remains. We know they were here on the banks of the river we now call Tallapoosa, and they would stay for many thousands of years through the time of transition into the period called Woodland.

Chapter 3
Woodland People

Many centuries passed since the Paleo and Archaic people first entered the Tallapoosa River Valley. Changes in their lifestyles occurred slowly, but by the Woodland period, several events and the increase in knowledge, made their daily routines less difficult. They were no longer the small bands of family groups that led a hunter-gatherer nomadic life, but were becoming larger groups of unrelated people who chose to make permanent homes. These people gathered for seasonal celebrations and trade and thus cultures were formed.

As mentioned in the previous chapter, the art of pottery making had arrived in the Tallapoosa River Valley. It is unclear if our people created pottery on their own or if it came by the route of diffusion. Diffusion was the method by which an invention or idea slowly moved from one place to another, sometimes taking years. Regardless, the Woodland people became very efficient in the art of pottery making. Since the cooking and storing of food was done by the women, they were undoubtedly the potters. Pottery was made from clay taken from the river bank, and must have been plentiful in our area. The first pottery was modeled much like what we did as children with our colorful clay. Plant fiber was used as a tempering or binding agent. Later, this was replaced by the coiled method and sand, gravel, shell, and even broken pieces of pottery were used to temper the clay.

Most pottery for everyday use was plain, but potters could also be very creative in the designs used to decorate their pots. Before the pot was placed in the hot coals, to be "fired" or hardened, the pottery would be stamped or incised. Natural objects such as brush, fiber cord, shells and even corncobs were used to create a beautiful work of art. The invention of pottery surely made life easier for the women, allowing them to cook food directly over a fire, and also provided a method of transporting and storing liquids. Dr. Knight found evidence of Woodland period pottery while excavating the Tuckabatchee area.

* * * * * * *

I cannot leave the subject of pottery without inserting a couple of my own pottery finding experiences on the Tallapoosa. Several years ago, my husband Randall and I were fishing on the second pond, as local folks call it, more correctly known as Yates Lake. We pulled the boat up to an island to have our lunch and the first thing I saw was a pottery sherd. My excitement likely equaled that of finding a piece of gold! We scratched around and found many more pieces.

I believe the site was used as a fishing camp dating back to the Woodland time period and was used off and on, and maybe continuously for the next two or three thousand years. Of course, every time we went fishing, and we like to fish, the island was a place of destination. We never found anything except pottery sherds, but some had quite elaborate designs. I have asked area archaeologists if they knew anything about the island, but so far no one has been able to tell me about the site. Although it is not as easy to find sherds now, we still go to that special place I call Pottery Island.

More recently, also while fishing, this time on the first pond, correctly known as Lake Thurlow. I stepped out of the boat and again found a pottery sherd. As with the first site, quite a lot of pottery has been found, more with beautiful designs made by an artisan from the long ago past. This site, which I call Pottery Spring, also has offered only pottery sherds. Like the first site, I believe it too was a fishing camp spanning several time periods.

* * * * * * *

Let's move on, now, to other inventions and changes for the Woodland people. The invention of the bow and arrow would slowly replace the throwing stick and the use of natural copper became widespread.

Apparently, the Woodland artisans became efficient with the use of copper. Various tools and personal ornaments such as ear spools, drilled beads, bracelets, and rolled-sheet beads were made. Many of these artifacts have been found on both sides of the Tallapoosa River, indicating our Woodland people had the use of copper. This was most likely a trade item coming from the Appalachian Mountains area. The Woodland people continued to make many of the same tools as did the Archaic people, only a little better. A new tool found at Woodland sites was the spade. Archaeologists believe the Woodland people might have actually begun to cultivate seeds, but we know the spades were used to dig post holes for their houses, to dig graves, and to move the soil for burial mound construction. Deceased people of the Woodland period were interred inside these mounds.

Some mounds contained one burial while others held several dozen. Construction of the mounds consisted of layers of clay or stone slabs separating the burials, indicating a mound could have been used over a period of time. Often, burials included tools and ornaments belonging to the deceased person. The mounds, often two or more together, were small and conical in shape, usually near a river or stream.

We know mounds dotted the landscape along the Tallapoosa, and most likely appeared in the Tuckabatchee area, but have not survived the passing of time. The effort and plans the Woodland people made to bury their dead was certainly the beginning of a new culture, a culture of a group of people with new ideas and new ideals. These people were called Mississippians.

Chapter 4
Mississippian People

The Mississippian people arrived at the highest culture achieved by Native Americans. Population increased, towns and villages became more like cities in some areas of the south, and along the Mississippi River. Places like Caokia, Etowah, and Moundville flourished and complex chiefdoms developed.

In the early years of the time period, simple forms of agriculture were practiced, and over time the Mississippians became efficient farmers. Corn or maize was the dominant crop, grown in abundance, and was an important economic factor. With the ability to grow food, the Mississippian people could make permanent homes, staying longer in one place.

One defining characteristic of the Mississippian time period was the construction of mounds, very large mounds. These mounds were not the smaller burial mounds of the Woodland period, but platform mounds, the largest being fifty to seventy-five feet in height and three-hundred to six-hundred feet at the base. Most of the larger ones were constructed in ceremonial towns. Hundreds of smaller ones, ranging from five to thirty feet in height and fifty to two-hundred fifty feet wide at the ground level, were scattered over the entire Southeast.

These earthen structures were constructed solely by hand! The town people carried thousands and thousands of baskets of dirt to make these massive structures. This was done over a period of time with the original mound starting off small. Over time more dirt was added, resulting in the mound becoming larger. These mounds were used as foundations for temples, council houses and for houses of town leaders.

Mississippian people perfected the art of making pottery, by not only making pots for domestic use, but for ceremonial and mortuary use as well. Bowls of various sizes and shapes with handles and loops, and long-necked bottles and pottery vessels in the form of animals or birds were made. Clay was used to form pipes, game discs, and other items. Beautiful elaborate designs, including serpents, birds, sun circles, the hand and the eye, were all symbols of the Southern ceremonial cult, appearing on many pottery masterpieces. Many of the same symbols and designs were also used by the Indians of Central America, more information on this later. Mississippian tools and ornaments were crafted to great perfection.

Mississippian burial customs included the practice of placing elaborate bowls and vessels, some containing food, with the deceased along with personal items. Some of the vessels would be deliberately "killed" or broken to allow the food substance to accompany the deceased to another world.

There is a burial practice unique to the Lower Tallapoosa and Upper Alabama River valley, and especially to the Talisi/Tuckabatchee area. This is the burial urn custom where the deceased was placed inside a large urn and covered with a flared or tuck rim top. The pottery urns were shell tempered with the top usually having the before-mentioned elaborate designs. Glass beads and other personal items of the deceased were placed inside the urn. This practice occurred during the late Mississippian period and continued to around 1700. This would account for the tremendous amount of pottery and the evidence of interred persons found at the Talisi site.

Mississippian people built permanent houses of the wattle and dobb style. Archaeological studies reveal post holes set a few feet apart, indicating the houses were square and were made with river cane and plastered with clay. They would have had thatched roofs made from palmetto branches. The floor would also be made of clay, with a center fire pit. The sides had bench-like seats called couches. The materials used to construct the houses, river cane, clay, and palmetto branches are still in abundance in the South and of course in the Tallassee area.

I have seen replicas of wattle and dobb houses and they actually looked like they would be comfortable, keeping the inhabitants warm and dry.

Several customs of the Mississippian people, such as divisions of authority, war and peace villages, the clan system, the harvest festival, and the black drink ceremony, as well as others, would still be observed several hundred years later in the historic time period.

As stated about previous time periods, most of the aforementioned information about the Mississippian people pertained primarily to the Southeast and to Alabama. Let's move now to the Lower Tallapoosa River Valley, more specific, the Talisi and Tuckabatchee areas.

While the region did not become one of the large mound metropolis cities, it did have Mississippian activity. Dr Knight, in his research of Tuckabatchee, stated there are two mounds dating to this period located on private property. In the early 1980s, when the study took place, the larger of the two mounds was about sixteen feet in height and sixty-by-eighty feet at the base. Unfortunately, the mound was being eroded by the river on the north side. The second mound is located about four-hundred feet west of the first. This one is much smaller, being less than five feet in height and about fifty feet at the base. This mound is more rounded and quite possibly may predate the larger one. It is also possible that little remains of the smaller mound due to the extensive cultivation and erosion in the area. Early maps show dozens of mounds, mainly about the size of the Tuckabatchee mounds, dotting the riverside between Tallassee and Wetumpka.

Dr. Knight thinks the actual Mississippian occupation of the Lower Tallapoosa Valley, which was known as the Shrine II Settlement, was made up of small, compact towns. Tuckabatchee was typical, being only about eleven acres in size. The one platform mound would have served as the center of town. This small Mississippian element would provide the growth that in the next couple of centuries would give rise to the much larger Tuckabatchee of the future.

* * * * * * *

On a sunny, but cold, cold Sunday afternoon in mid February of 2012, Randall and I decided to visit the Tuckabatchee mound. We had over the years, been to many sites and locations on the banks of the Tallapoosa, but never had been to the mound together. We knew it was there, but not its precise location. We also knew the mound was on private property, but we had obtained permission to visit the site. I had actually seen the mound back in the fall of 2011, in conjunction with a Native American retreat I was fortunate to attend. So, I knew where it was, well not exactly. We both knew the general location from the description in Dr. Knight's book and I had, after all been to it before. How hard can it be to find a large mound on the river bank? One might be surprised. When we turned off Alabama Highway 229 South onto the tiny dirt road that runs directly through the heart of Tuckabatchee, I immediately became excited, no, more than excited. Since my childhood, each time I traveled down that little road I experience a special feeling. The road leads to a place, to me, that transcends time, a place where thousands of native people had lived for thousands of years. I feel their presence. No, I am not crazy. Their spirit is undoubtedly a part of me.

Let's return to the search for the mound. The little road with several turns and forks extends well over a mile to the river. When we reached the fork, we knew which way to turn and I was pretty sure I could take us right to it. After riding back and forth in the designated area, to no avail, we got out and walked into the woods next to the river, still no sign of the mound. As it turned out, I had taken us too far up river. If it was not there, then it must be down river. Then, just around a couple of little bends in the road along the tree line, there was the mound, complete with a path leading to it.

The large platform mound was pitted with holes dug by pothunters, who had attempted to seek treasures from the past. I think probably in vain, as platform mounds were just that, a platform for a temple or a house for a chief. Most likely the mound did not contain any artifacts of value. It was a sad sight to see the mound defaced by unscrupulous individuals who cared nothing for the people who had sat atop and viewed the surrounding village. As Dr. Knight mentioned, the north side bordered the river with only a few feet separating the towering mound from the rapidly flowing Tallapoosa. The mound likely dates CA (meaning circa or approximate date), 1400-1500, which means it was constructed in the late Mississippian period.

Randall and I looked for the smaller second mound, but could not positively say we found it. I think that mound has vanished just as the people who had built it hundreds of years ago. I did see remnants of them being there, as the little roadway was covered with tiny pieces of pottery sherds. Yes, I did take a few pieces home, just so I will have something to remind me of our trip to find the Tuckabatchee mound.

* * * * * * *

The Mississippian culture would continue to thrive, reaching new heights filled with abundant riches and wealth for some. Others would not experience this degree of wealth and in fact would be condemned to serve chiefdom hierarchies, thus forming a class system.

As I stated earlier, maize or corn was the main food substance for the Mississippian people and was grown in great quantities. It seems the chieftain expected a portion of the crop from each family to be given to him. This was used to enhance his wealth and also used to provide food for the village people in time of need. This observation about food and the class system in my opinion answers the question asked by many, what happened to the Mississippian people? After the tremendous heights achieved, with large populations and wealth, the great Mississippian culture seemed to collapse very quickly. Obviously, food was not the issue, nor was there evidence of a large scale war or of a pandemic disease. So, what happened and where did they go?

Even though the chiefdom was based on family kinship, as time went by and families grew there was less and less kin to the chief and less benefit for the bottom echelon. I think these people got tired of serving someone else, and just gathered their individual families and moved away from the large village complex, thus eroding the Mississippian culture.

The Mississippian culture or remnants of it would last until the early 1500s. Even the ever-changing cycle of events in their lives could not prepare the Mississippian people for the introduction to a new race, the Europeans. After Columbus discovered America in 1492, there would be a few random explorers to enter the country. Most were not here long and many had no contact with the native people, but some did.

Legend has it one explorer may have entered Alabama in the areas of current Talladega or Sylacauga, possibly a Viking. Little information is known so quite possibly, this is only a legend.

Native people, and rightly so, had great fear of these unfamiliar beings with white skin and strange behavior. The natives must have thought they had encountered some sort of gods. Early explorers were primarily here for just that, to explore, but they brought with them the precursor of destruction for the native people, diseases that would almost annihilate their race over the next century or two. They would continue their way of life, even though the Mississippian culture had begun to fade. And then one day … there was DeSoto.

Chapter 5
DeSoto and His Entourage

Hernando DeSoto.

Every child who has studied Alabama history knows who DeSoto was, but few know his true story. It is much too complicated and controversial for me to tell here, even though I've read every word of The DeSoto Cronicles. However, I do have my opinions about the explorer.

DeSoto, with his entourage of over six-hundred men from all walks of life, their horses and hogs, first entered America in May of 1539, near Tampa Bay. For the next four years this group of intruders would travel over the southeastern part of what would become the United States. He saw the Indians in their native environment and observed their cultural practices. Seeing the simplicity of the Indian's lives, he wreaked havoc, destruction, and death on the native people.

Near the end of his journey, after discovering the Mississippi River, DeSoto came down with a fever which was then spread to the natives. He died and was buried in the muddy river, forever remaining in the land he came to plunder of its great wealth, but instead met his demise.

The big question here is whether or not DeSoto came to our Tallassee. Of all the southeastern States traversed by the DeSoto entourage, Alabama has pursued the route most extensively. In fact, Alabama was one of the first to actually plot the route of the expedition, but State archaeologists and historians agree the least on where he traveled. DeSoto entered from north Georgia, spending six months in Alabama, traveling over five-hundred miles on the native inhabitant's trails. He and his band of soldiers fought the biggest battle of the entire expedition here, the Battle of Mavilla. No one knows the exact location of Mavilla. Recently, some archaeologists have speculated that Mavilla was likely located near

Gee's Bend on the Alabama River in Wilcox County.

It is documented that the expedition did visit Talisi in September of 1540.

There is on one of the DeSoto maps a Talisi in current Talladega County, one near Selma in Dallas County, and of course the Talisi on the Tallapoosa. Many historians, including Albert Pickett, author of the History of Alabama, think without a doubt the renowned explorer visited our Talisi on the Tallapoosa. There are many who think, and I have concluded as well, that he did not.

After entering our state from Georgia, Hernando DeSoto traveled down a big river. Earlier I stated the Tallapoosa begins in Georgia, but only as a small creek, which would not have been considered a large river. I think he followed the Coosa, which is a big river as it exits Georgia and the Talisi he visited was in Talladega County. That is not to say that some smaller division of the main expedition might have come close to our Talisi. The town of Eclectic, which is fifteen miles northwest of Tallassee in Elmore County, claims DeSoto camped in a grove of trees there. In reality, no one really knows for sure the exact route of DeSoto or to which Talisi he came. Of course, at this point, it really does not matter. History reveals the intrusion of the DeSoto expedition and other explorers only succeeded in bringing disease and destruction to the native people in areas far reaching the actual routes.

Chapter 6
The Muscogee
From Where Did They Come?

We know many, some nameless, groups or bands of native people had been in the Talisi area for thousands of years, but what about the people we call Muscogee? They had not always been here. It is generally known the Muscogee came from the Red River area of Texas, and before that, Mexico. Yes, I said Mexico. I have thought for many years that our Indians had connections with those from Mexico, the Maya and Aztecs.

Pickett, in his *History of Alabama*, gives the migration story of the Muscogee to Alabama. His information was obtained from Le Clerc Milfort, a Frenchman who lived in the Creek Nation in 1776. Milfort spent much time with older Creeks, who spoke of their ancestors and of the traditions of where they came. Other theories exist, but this one seems logical to me.

Pickett states in 1519, Spanish troops led by Hernando Cortez landed in Vera Cruz, Mexico. To combat this invasion, Montezuma, leader of the Aztecs, assembled forces from all parts of his empire. At that time the Muscogee had formed a separate republic in northwest Mexico, and were asked to aid in the battle. Something happened that had never occurred before, Montezuma and his armies were defeated. He was killed and his empire overthrown. The Muscogee, having lost many warriors, were unwilling to live in a conquered country. Searching for a new land, the entire group moved north and east to the Red River area. Here they spent several years in peace, but eventually a new group invaded their territory. This group too, would have future ties to our State; in fact, the State would be named for them. They were the Alabama, who also arrived from the west.

Around 1527, the Alabama attacked the Muscogee, killing several. The Muscogee left their town, pursuing the Alabama, seeking revenge. This chain of events, with first one and then the other attacking, continued for one-hundred years. The two groups moved north to the Missouri River, then Ohio, Wabash, Yazoo, and the Tennessee. Around 1620, the Alabama reached the river named for them, settled there, and built permanent homes. Still unsure of the whereabouts of the unrelenting Muscogee, some Alabama warriors went back to see if their foe was still in pursuit. They were, and again they fought. This time the Muscogee prevailed, and liking the area, decided it would be a good place to live. Without opposition, the Muscogee took possession of the land on the Alabama River and also that along the Coosa and Tallapoosa. The unfortunate Alabama fled, taking refuge with the Choctaws and other tribes. They would in the future make peace with the Muscogee, becoming a part of their confederacy and again making their home on the Alabama River.

This sequence of events established the dominance and power the mighty Muscogee would experience for the next two-hundred and fifty years. They pushed eastward, claiming territory all the way to the east coast, absorbing smaller tribes, thus forming the Great Muscogee Confederacy.

Chapter 7
Home At Last

The Muscogee Confederacy continued to thrive in the new land and their population grew. Some moved on to the Okmulgee, Oconee and Savannah Rivers for a period of time. In 1715, the Yamasee and the Apalachee, two powerful and war-like tribes who lived near the eastern coast, avenged mistreatment by British colonists. This event was called the Yamasee War and caused quite a problem for the colonists. Even though the Muscogee were not active participants in the war, many lived near the region and some of the Apalachee settled near the Muscogee after the uprising. A fear of reprisal from the English prompted the Muscogee to move back to the Chattahoochee and Tallapoosa River areas. This is the time period when the English began to refer to the Muscogee as Creeks. A group of Muscogee living on Ogeechee Creek in east-central Georgia was simply called Creeks by traders.

Around this time, a new group of people arrived on the lower Tallapoosa, the Tuckabatcha. Sound confusing? The Tuckabatcha were not of the original Muscogee group. They came from the Ohio River area after having been nearly destroyed by the Northern Iroquois and Huron. The Muscogee, always seeking to add to their confederacy, allowed the Tuckabatcha to settle here. Some think the Tuckabatcha's first settlement was on the east bank of the Tallapoosa River.

Here will be a good time to examine the origin and meaning of our two towns and also that of the magnificent river. Let's start with the river. As stated in the beginning of my story, the Tallapoosa begins as a small stream in west Georgia. I wonder how the State of Georgia can benefit from such a tiny stream in the 21st century water war with Alabama and Florida. Once in Alabama the Tallapoosa begins its mighty rush to join the Coosa, forming the graceful Alabama. It finishes its journey entering the Gulf of Mexico. Early maps show various names for the Tallapoosa, including Locushatchee or Locust River, from the locust trees which apparently grew on the banks. My favorite is Okwhuske or Oakfuskee, or sometimes called Fawn River. Then finally Tallapoosa, possibly named for an ancient tribe. The word is actually from the Choctaw, meaning tali-rock and pushi-pulverized or simply put, "little rock." Anyone who has ever been on the Tallapoosa River knows that the rocks are definitely not "little," giving reason to think that maybe another name might apply, Cat-In-The-Cane-Break. This probably comes from the vast amount of river cane that still grows along the river and for the big cats, the panther, cougar and the mountain lion that roamed the area.

* * * * * * *

I have a great love for the Tallapoosa and feel some sort of special tie to the river. Of course, it is beautiful as it flows alternately from slow and serene to the mighty rush of current over the rocks that lie just beneath the surface forming numerous rapids.

My husband and I have spent many, many hours on the Tallapoosa and in fact as I write this, I look out over the river, as we are blessed to live just above the great falls. If one listens very closely, especially down the river near the sites of the villages, it's almost as though the voices of the past speak. Fanciful, I know, but the Tallapoosa River is special and that is why so many people have lived here for so many years.

* * * * * * *

Before moving on to the village names, I need to mention a little more about the Tallapoosa. Extending for three miles above the falls, the river was one half mile wide and the entire area was in shoals. At different times, deer and then cattle and horses ate moss from the rocks which was a source of salt. Above the falls were four islands which were planted in corn for hundreds of years. An 1863 map shows the names given to the islands as Buzzard, Cat and Long. I have never read or heard the name of the fourth smaller island. I wonder what the Indian names were. The islands are no longer visible, being under water since the construction of Thurlow Dam in the early 1930s. The locations can be found with a depth finder, and on rare occasions when the lake level is low, stickups can be seen from the islands.

Now to the great falls. What a spectacular site that must have been. They were more than fifty feet wide and nearly a half mile in length and divided into two channels. The eastern channel fell forty feet in fifty yards and the western fell twenty feet in about ten yards. The large granite boulders were divided into square blocks, looking as if human hands had formed them, instead of being formed by an act of nature. The view from the Benjamin Fitzpatrick Bridge today is still amazing, but if one goes to the road beneath the bridge, some of the former greatness can still be seen.

Now, we move on to the villages and their names. We know for thousands of years, dating back to the Paleo and Archaic time periods, the banks of the Tallapoosa and its many creeks and streams feeding the river were occupied in early times by nameless groups, and then by names of villages and people that have long been forgotten. These people were simply called the Tallapoosees, then later on the Talisis and the Tuckabatchees. There is some confusion as to which of the two towns were occupied first. I think the occupation of each came fairly close together and the settling of the first created reason for the second. Town location only adds to the confusion. The fact is many towns had the same name and would often relocate to different areas. This also applies to our towns, Talisi and Tuckabatchee.

Chapter 8
Talisi

Since I don't know — and I'm not sure anyone else really knows — which town was settled first, Talisi or Tuckabatchee, I'll begin with Talisi. Both towns appear at their present locations on very early maps of Spanish and French origin. Spanish documents mention Talashe as early as 1597. Could this be our Talisi?

Following the many twist and bends of the Tallapoosa, Talisi was located about five miles below the falls on the east bank of the river. Maps and many historians place the village at the confluence of the Euphapee Creek in present Macon County. Actually, the site is about one-half mile from the upper bank of the Euphapee and just below a little creek called Ashurst Mill Creek. The Indian word for the latter creek is we-lar-hee or Yellow Water Creek. The water still has a yellowish, brackish tint, probably due to the slow movement of the stream.

The Talisi site is on a hill, the elevation being two-hundred feet above sea level. From information supplied by my late father-in-law, Talisi was the only site in the area not under water when the river flooded. He recalled from his childhood, that small animals and snakes would converge there to escape the raging river. This is probably the reason for the selection of this as a village site since the hilltop never floods.

Talisi, Talase, Talechys, to name a few of the different spellings, in accordance to which nationality did the spelling. I think it was pronounced just as we pronounce it today, Tallassee (TAL-uh-see). I wish the early white settlers had not changed the spelling, but it's a couple of hundred years too late to return to the original spelling as some locals have suggested.

The most common meaning for Talisi is a compound of the Creek word 'talwa,' meaning town and 'hasi,' meaning old. Also, Tal-e-see is equivalent to 'talofa' town and 'isi,' taken or captured. I think both apply, Talisi is both an "old town" and at one point a "captured town." It has been called big or old Talisi to differentiate between it and Little Talisi on the Coosa River near Wetumpka. Some historians refer to Talisi as 'Tulsa,' probably a name used in the late historical period. When removed to Indian Territory or Oklahoma, the Creeks took their town name with them and Tulsa was the name taken by the Talisis. Tallassee, Alabama and Tulsa, Oklahoma are today known as sister cities. The word 'Tulsa' means 'Council House.' Old timers refer to the Talisi site as "Townhouse Hill." Townhouse would be a derivative of council house, which was a meeting place for town leaders. I will speak more about that later.

* * * * * * *

Townhouse Hill was the site referred to in my introduction, the place where I picked up dozens of little blue and black trade beads and the place where my intense interest in Native Americans began. We visited the site many times during my childhood and as an adult, my husband and I too have spent countless, wonderful hours at Townhouse. It has been many years now since we were there, but I can still fondly remember the heat from the summer sun and the smell of the river and the pungent earth that was once the home of a different people, so many years ago. Each time we left, I would always look back, knowing there would come a time when I couldn't return, that one day Townhouse Hill would not be the same. It is gone now, the property was purchased by someone from out of town and a huge hunting lodge was built right on top of the village site, right on top of the homes where "The People of the Townhouse" lived and the places where they died and were buried. Yes, it is gone now and mostly forgotten, mentioned only in books where very little is written and only a few will ever read.

Turning now to the archaeological facts about Talisi, to my knowledge, the Talisi site has never been as extensively studied or excavated as the Tuckabatchee site. I remember hearing that back in the 1930s, archeologists from Auburn University did do a small scale excavation, but I have never found any further information. I would assume artifacts found are still in possession of Auburn University. I do know that over the years, many artifacts have been removed from Townhouse Hill. Sadly to say, I recall hearing that at one point a bulldozer was used to scrape the surface and that burials were uncovered. I find this reprehensible and it deeply saddens me. My husband Randall and I only surface hunt for artifacts.

* * * * * * *

One very cold February day, back in the early 1980s, Randall and I were at Townhouse Hill. There had been frequent rain and freezing temperatures causing the ground to spew and then sink. One such area contained the remains of an indigenous person. It was obvious that someone had been there before us as the remains were scattered in an attempt to find artifacts. Burials often included personal ornaments, tools and weapons of the deceased person. Since I had always wanted to be an archaeologist, I was not squeamish about finding human remains. I calmly picked up the bones and put them back into the grave and re-interred the remains of a person that I would have loved to have met. It might have been silly, but I did say that I was sorry. I'm sure that many Indian graves have been unearthed, but I don't know how many people would go to the trouble or take the time to re-bury the occupants.

On another occasion, we were walking in a field upstream from the Talisi site when Randall stepped on a round metal object and picked it up. It was encrusted with dried mud and he thought it was a part from a plow or tractor. I immediately picked up a large red bead and said, "This did not come from a tractor!" We looked more carefully at the object we had just found and discovered it to be a bell. We then noticed more objects just barely visible. We did scratch around a little with a stick and to our amazement; we had found a grave site. The grave had been uncovered and scattered by the extensive plowing that had taken place for decades. We found several more bells, the larger being one to one and one-half inches in circumference and having the letter "K" stamped on the bottom. The bells were identified later by an archaeologist as being rumbler bells. The bells were most likely strung on a harness and placed around a horse or cows neck for the jingling sound. At times these bells were used as ornaments worn during native dance ceremonies, and even today, to hear the jingle prompts instant goose bumps. Seriously!

Other items found included, a large brass bell, with the clapper missing, brass side plates from three rifles, a copper needle, a small copper container, musket flints, brass buttons, pottery sherds, river rocks, many black beads, blue beads and a few red beads. Also, parts of the skeletal remains of the owner of the mentioned items, which was as before, promptly re-interred. The artifacts found were in surprisingly good condition, considering the time that had lapsed since the Creek man had lived and used them. Judging by the type of items found, the man was most likely affluent and I think the time period of his burial was between 1780 and 1830, perhaps closer to the latter. We thought the area contained many more undisturbed graves, but we could not confirm it. We did in fact, contact the University of Alabama and informed them of our find. They did identify the bells but never came to the site. If we had not stumbled, literally, on the site, the artifacts would have been scattered and the information that I pieced together would not exist. A short time after that, the site was found by someone else. We heard the site was looted and destroyed, apparently with the landowner's knowledge. That was a shame. Valuable information could have been obtained.

* * * * * * *

Another written account was given by Dr. J. M. Glenn, a Methodist minister who served in Tallassee in the 1930s. He relates a story I have heard before. During construction of the gas pipeline that runs just below Tallassee, workers unearthed a grave. The grave was located on the east side of the river, about a mile south of Stone Creek. The skeletal remains of an Indian as well as his dog were found. His gun and hatchet were included in the grave as if he might need them again. The Indians fully believed in another life after this life.

I am sure others have found graves and remains of Tallassee's indigenous people. It is very possible many more remain hidden beneath the grassy slopes of lawns, or enclosed forever under factory floors and underneath the asphalt of busy highways. We know for sure an old Indian burial ground, which was possibly the final resting place of early white setters as well, is located beneath Barnett Boulevard in present day downtown Tallassee. The area in front of the current bank, extending across the street to include the old water tank vicinity, was once sacred ground. Supposedly, the white burials were re-interred at Rose Hill Cemetery when the road was constructed, but I'm not sure about the Indians. Someday while driving along Barnett, think about the times of long ago and the people who lived here … and the place where they were buried.

Chapter 9
Tuckabatchee

Let's move back down the river now to our other village, Tuckabatchee, Tukabatchi or Tiquipache which are three of about a dozen ways to spell it. Again, the spelling differs depending on the nationality, whether French, Spanish or the Native Americans, whoever is pronouncing the town's name at that particular time period. I like Tuckabatchee, the spelling most commonly used today. As for the meaning, like Talisi, there is more than one. The first meaning is Talwa-fatcho-sigo, "incorrect town" or "one not sufficiently strict." The Creek elements are 'talwa,' which means town, 'fachi,' meaning "right or straight" and 'sigo,' "not." The other name, which is older, is Is-po-cogee, which means "town of survivors," from the Creek word isipokok' or "I put a wrap around myself." This information comes from the book *Indian Place Names in Alabama*, written by William A. Read, a neat little book that I have referred to often.

Amos J. Wright, Jr. in his book, *Historic Indian Towns in Alabama, 1540-1838*, states that "Tiquipache" appears on a list of upper Creek towns in 1675, and it also shows up on a 1686 map. Like Talisi, we know Tuckabatchee had been occupied for thousands of years, but was not known by that name until a later time period.

Tuckabatchee was located across the river from Talisi, which is the information given by most books. That is true, but the difference can vary by a mile or maybe two, according to the time period. The many twists and turns of the Tallapoosa make the positioning of these towns a little difficult to pinpoint. I doubt that many of the authors of books have floated down the river and actually gone from site to site as I have.

The nucleus of early Tuckabatchee was probably just up-river from Talisi. At one point, Tuckabatchee was a vast settlement. Dr. John Cottier of Auburn University stated the town at its height extended from the flat just below the present Southside Middle School, all the way to the great bend of the river. It has been said Tuckabatchee was three to six miles below the falls. That too would be correct, depending on the time period.

Unlike Talisi, much has been written about Tuckabatchee and many various accounts of the town and her people. Included is the fact that Tuckabatchee was one of the four founding sticks, or towns, and the mother town of the Creek Confederacy. In the next chapter we will take some time to visit Tuckabatchee before it acquired that prestigious title. Let's go back to the time period of 1600 to about 1715, a period archaeologists call the Atasi Culture or Phase.

Chapter 10
Atasi Culture at Tuckabatchee

Archaeologists sometimes will base an entire culture on evidence obtained from the pottery of the time period. The Atasi, or at times spelled Autossee, culture was first reported by Dr. Peter Brannon from pottery excavated from the Atasi site. Atasi was a town about five miles down river from Tuckabatchee at the confluence of Calebee Creek and the Tallapoosa River. The two towns of Tuckabatchee and Atasi would in the future be linked together by more than just pottery sherds, but that will be disclosed later.

By the Atasi Phase, only cultural remnants of the Mississippian period remained. Gone was the construction of mounds, in fact by the 1600s, only the oldest members of the town had any memory of their original use, or who the people were who had built them.

From Dr. Knight's cultural research assessment of Tuckabatchee, he states that the Atasi phase occupation was abundant with substantial growth. The village that would in the future be known as Tuckabatchee became extensive with traditional Creek houses made from wattle, which was woven river cane, and daub, or clay. For this particular phase, excavations were made southeast from Tallassee's old Reeves Airport runway, where much evidence relating to the Atasi phase was unearthed. Dr. Knight's excavation revealed both circular and square floor plans. This information was obtained by determining the arrangement of post holes and hearths.

Atasi phase pottery was very pretty and meticulously made. The incised designs were bold and wide spaced and corn cobs were often used as engraving tools. Sand or grit and occasional shell were used as the tempering agent. Tempering agents helped bind the clay together as the vessels were being formed and fired. The most common vessel types included the flared-rimmed jar and carinated or symmetrically formed bowls.

By now you know, I enjoy finding pottery, and I save every piece. I have buckets full of pottery sherds and the really special pieces have designs. I have been able to classify several sherds as being from the Atasi phase.

Evidence of the lithic industry included small triangular arrowheads, small edged tools, end scrappers and shaft drills. Materials used were coastal plain chert, quartz and petrified wood. Dr. Knight and his group found aboriginal artifacts which included clay pipes, clay beads and mullers which are concave stones used for grinding corn. Fragments found included discordials or round flat rocks used in a game called chunky. A schist slab, which was possibly a hoe, was the only agricultural tool found at the site.

Even though archaeologists think the Talisi-Tuckabatchee area was not visited by European traders prior to 1686, much evidence of their trade goods have been documented. Personal items, such as the colorful blue, white, black and turquoise glass beads, of various sizes, were found in abundance. Small brass ornaments including pendants, tubular beads and silver ornaments were found, but with less frequency. If the traders had yet to arrive in the area, how then did the indigenous people possess the European trade goods? The answer is simple. The Spanish had by that time colonized coastal Florida. Some of the soldiers or missionaries made forages into the interior, perhaps making contact with Indian people of distant tribes. Those Indians would then connect with others and this process continued, all the while, trading occurred until eventually the people of the Tallapoosa River Valley acquired the trinkets of this trade. After discovering this source of trade items, some of the Tallapoosa people possibly traveled to the coast to deal directly with the Spanish.

Another item of interest introduced by the Spanish at this time was the domestic peach. While the peach did not change the normal food source and supply, it did add a new variety to their diet and would in future years become a status symbol of wealth. While on the subject of food, I need to mention the plant and animal remains identified in Dr. Knight's account. Walnuts, hickory nuts, wild peaches, squash rind and maize were some of the plants found. Deer, raccoon, opossum, squirrel, fish and turtle were the animal food supply eaten by the Atasi phase people.

This new avenue of obtaining luxury items through trade during the Atasi period made a change in the domestic economy of the Talisi-Tuckabatchee people. Another change would be the introduction, not of a new food or material for daily use, but the appearance of a new and different people.

Chapter 11
Shawnee Newcomers
and the Tuckabatchee Plates

Many historians think that Tuckabatchee was actually a Shawnee town. The Shawnee, a northern tribe that seemed to migrate from place to place, relocating frequently, were almost destroyed by the Iroquois and Huron. Sometime around the year 1675, the Shawnee asked the Muscogee for protection from their northern enemies. The Muscogee in the continuing effort to increase the size of their confederacy took the Shawnee in and gave them land in the center of their nation. A new town was formed at this time, possibly from the Shawnee joining with the existing Muscogee, to create the "incorrect town" or "town of survivors," from which Tuckabatchee gets its name.

George Stiggins, a man of Muscogee-Natchez-White ancestry, who lived among the Tuckabatchee, stated that the Shawnee solidified the pack between the two tribes with a gift. The gift consisted of pipes, wampum belts, a ceremonial war club and the Tuckabatchee Plates.

The Tuckabatchee Plates are a mysterious collection of rectangular and circular copper and brass plates, inscribed with strange symbols. The Muskogee held them in great reverence and believed they were connected with mystical beings and contained supernatural power. The plates were displayed in ceremonial rituals only, and when not in use, were carefully guarded.

I am intrigued by the Tuckabatchee Plates and their origin. If Stiggins' theory is correct, where did the Shawnee get the plates? Another, I think highly romanticized theory, is that the plates were obtained from the DeSoto expedition. As I explained in the beginning, and many archaeologists and historians have the same professional opinions, DeSoto did not visit the Talisi-Tuckabatchee area. Thus, I do not think the plates came from that expedition, unless some of the Talisi-Tuckabatchee people came in contact with DeSoto outside of the region.

Several of the plates appear to be of aboriginal manufacture and are made from hammered native copper. Another theory is that the plates were found in the ground placed in burials by earlier people. Other artifacts resembling the Tuckabatchee plates were also found down river at Atasi, as well as at a site near the falls in 1930 by the Alabama Anthropological Society. Dr. Knight in his archaeological survey of Tuckabatchee states, the Shawnee may have found the plates while digging for clay to build their houses and then offered them to the Muscogee with the other items to consummate their alliance.

No one will ever know for sure the source of the Tuckabatchee plates; but the fact is they do exist and that they came from Tuckabatchee makes them special. They continued to be held in reverence and esteem by the Tuckabatchee people for the next 150 years, up to the time of removal. In fact, during the trip to Indian Territory, the plates were carried, wrapped in buckskins, by Creeks of impeccable moral character. They walked one in front of the other, in a solemn religious manner, a mile in advance of the others, only talking among themselves. To this day, the Tuckabatchee Plates are still used in ceremonies and serve as a reminder to the Muscogee people in Oklahoma of their past and from where they came.

Chapter 12
Tallapoosa Culture at Tuckabatchee
1715-1780

Cultural change did not occur quickly for the people of the Tallapoosa River Valley. In fact, decades and even centuries would pass with the children still living the same simple life style as their ancestors. The early to mid years of the 18th century were no exception. Actually, this may have been one of the more tranquil time periods for the Muscogee people. The river and river valley supplied ample food for the growing confederacy. Of course, there was occasional warfare, mostly just quick raids and retaliations for some wrong done to a family member.

An important factor during this peaceful time period experienced by the Talisi-Tuckabatchee was the absence of the white man, who would eventually arrive to take their homeland. That event would come in the near future. After having lost thousands of their number to disease spread by European explorers two centuries earlier, populations of the indigenous people had again increased. Let's take a closer look at how the Talisi and Tuckabatchee lived in the early Tallapoosa Phase.

Villages of this time period were constructed in a definite pattern. Household structures were organized and arranged around a central compound or courtyard. The term most often used for this village arrangement was the square ground as defined by botanist and adventurer William Bartram who traversed the south, including the Tallapoosa River Valley area in 1776 and 1777.

In Creek culture, much loyalty and devotion was expressed for their talwa or town. Residents of a particular town considered themselves to be the same as their town, a Tuckabatchee or a Talisi. The Tuckabatchee talwa, as with all Creek towns, was organized around the public square.

The square consisted of four open rectangular wooden sheds, all facing each other. Adjacent to the square was the great town or council house, called by the Creeks a chokofa, a large circular building used in winter and during inclement weather and capable of holding dozens of people. These were the areas where elders and beloved men would gather to conduct business and to discuss affairs of the town, to socialize, to drink the black drink called ascee, to pass the pipe, to gossip and to tell tall tales of past heroic deeds. This was the domain of the Creek man.

No one can precisely identify where the Tuckabatchee square ground was, but using the information and maps that I have studied, as well as local legends, I think I can calculate to a fairly close location. Leaving Tallassee on Highway 229 south, and using the GKN-Aerospace plant and the old Reaves Airport runway as reference points, look toward the southeast. Look out over the vast field which in the early fall is white with cotton. Follow the tree line as it curves with the river and there about two miles from the roadway, two-hundred years ago, would have been the bustling town square of Tuckabatchee.

Individual households were smaller versions of the town square. Each household consisted of four small buildings organized around a small square. One of the houses would be for winter living quarters and activities while one would be arranged for summer life. The other two structures were used for storage of food and personal belongings. The small domestic sites were occupied by married couples and their children. This nucleus family was a Creek tradition and not influenced by European contact; however a factor that did influence Creek society was the emergence of the trader.

As previously mentioned, the Talisi and Tuckabatchee had no direct contact with the European trader until the late 1600s and early 1700s. At that time traders were invited to come. What a period of excitement this must have been for our people. I can imagine the scene:

With the sun shinning brightly, a trader, maybe the first white man ever seen by the women and children, walked into Tuckabatchee town from the Creek trading path, arriving from the direction of the rising sun, from a place called Charles Town. His dress and appearance would have seemed strange, a combination of European and Indian clothing, a colorful turban wrapped around his head, his face covered in hair and his skin fair. He speaks some Muscogee or Choctaw. A large crowd of Tuckabatchee people gather around with the women and children trying to get a closer view of the man. He resembled a modern day Santa Claus with a bright red blanket flung over his shoulder. The contents of his blanket created even more excitement. After all of the formal greetings and possibly the pipe passed, the trader spread his blanket on the square ground. What the Tuckabatchee people saw was truly an amazing sight. There were hundreds of colorful beads, which quickly became a prized possession of the Muscogee and mirrors, knives, bells and axes just to name some of the other items this strange visitor had to offer. He passed out a few of the beads or maybe a mirror or two to some of the women and children, in an attempt to make a good impression. The men were his primary customers, the hunters who could supply the deer skins and hides of other animals, items that would make the trader much money.

This may have been the first trader to enter Tuckabatchee town, but his successors would be many. Over the next hundred years or so, the trader would be a constant in the area. The excitement the people experienced for these simple cheap trinkets, turned into dependence, a dependence that would change their lives and their culture and almost cost them the identity of the Muscogee Nation. This was a huge price to pay for little trinkets. If they had only known, would they have acted differently? Probably, not. This was their destiny. We will come back to the trader and his effects later.

Artifact data recovered at the Tuckabatchee site, from the Tallapoosa Phase, reveal ceramics were similar in technique for food preparation, serving and storing as in the Atasi time period. Most of the change was stylistic, with smaller vessel size and the lack of shell tempering. Considerable amount of European artifact material was found including fragments of thick, dark green glass. These containers were commonly called rum bottles, but during this period, rum was imported in casks from the West Indies. The bottles were most likely English and contained wine or brandy.

By the mid 1700s, the beautiful greenstone celts had been replaced by iron hoes and axes. Of course, these items made day to day life easier, but in doing so, lost was a centuries-old technique of making simple stone into a work of art. At this point in time, the trade gun had not yet replaced the bow and arrow, but evidence of gun parts were found as well as iron items. The ancient lithic industry of arrow point crafting continued. The points were smaller than those made during the Atasi period and many were still made from beautiful chert. Brass projectile points were found, a definite precursor of the upcoming change in weaponry. Rolled copper points had been used by the indigenous people of the Tuckabatchee and Talisi areas for decades. Pipes were still primarily manufactured by local aboriginal people using steatite and kaolin, which in simple terms was stone and clay. During this time period, trade silver in the form of jewelry was worn by both men and women. The women wore silver earrings, bracelets and hair pins, while the men favored silver arm bands. Some began to mix European style clothing with traditional native attire. The ever popular glass trade beads were still worn in abundance and continued to be a fashion statement for Native Americans.

Life continued to be good for the Talisi and Tuckabachee people in the middle of the 18th century. The European traders and their trade goods had affected their lifestyle in a positive way, up until this point.

The introduction of the iron hatchet and pot may have simplified and made their daily life easier, but this too was the beginning of a change that in the future would be detrimental. I think this would have been the time period I would have most liked to visit, if that were possible, a time when their culture was still native and had not been totally changed by the greed of the white race. Time was growing short for the Talisi and Tuckabatchee people, although they did not realize it.

Chapter 13
Late Tallapoosa Culture at Tuckabatchee
1780-1836

By the 1780s, in the late Tallapoosa time period, European influence increased. Before we get to that change and its affect, let's take a look at how the river valley people continued to live during that period. The animal food supply was still primarily deer, bear and other smaller animals. The river was abundant with fish, mussels and turtles. They continued to gather wild plants such as hickory nuts and maypop seeds. Vast fields of corn were common with squash and beans being plentiful.

Dr. Knight and his team excavated underground, trash filled storage bins or midden pits from the Tuckabatchee site. These were basin-shaped and seemed to be a new feature for this time period. This provided a method of storing and preserving foods.

Although our people may have had the use of European trade pots, pottery was still made and used in abundance. The method of making pottery had changed very little from earlier years, still showing aesthetic beauty. Artifacts found show the carinated bowl and deep flare-rimmed jars were among the most popular types.

As in the early Tallapoosa period the lithic industry did continue, but more and more aboriginal tools were replaced by iron. At this time major changes began to take place. Houses changed from the traditional wattle and daub style, to those resembling the log cabin of the white man. Food production changed and Talisi and Tuckabatchee people began to own cattle and hogs, raising many to trade or sell.

By the late 1700s, strong evidence of European contact was visible. In order to provide his family with the luxury items which now seemed essential, owning the flintlock musket was an absolute necessity for the

Creek man. With new habits and ways of living, the Talisi and Tuckabatchee people were becoming acculturated.

The time it took to enter into their new lifestyle — was not a long span of time — instead it was very brief. Before moving on to their new lifestyle I should cover some of the more important cultural habits and the way our people lived before the European influence, the events and occasions that brought them happiness and others that brought them pain. Let's begin with the religious beliefs of the Muscogee people.

The cultural world of the Muscogee was one of endurance and perseverance, of having the ability to accept the challenge of survival through out time. Their belief in the Giver of Breath, the Great Spirit was a constant and a presence of which they were ever aware. The Muscogee believed the Great Spirit was the Supreme Creator and all in their world came from this creator.

They worshipped no idols, but showed great reverence to the sun and moon, understanding that these too were provided for their comfort by the Great Spirit. The Muscogee did not have a special time to worship, but in words and actions did offer their thanks and praise daily. The Muscogee believed that every creature — man, animal, even the inanimate object — had a spirit or soul and rewards or punishment would be granted in some future state of existence. They believed there were three worlds: this world, the upper world and the lower world. The Muscogee people believed in visions, dreams, trances and supernatural powers. Being very superstitious, they were spirit haunted, fearing ghosts, witches and other curious creatures. If a spirit was offended, an act of purification must occur to appease the spirit. Each day began with a ritual bath in the river or stream, more to purify the soul than to cleanse the body. The act of purification and renewal escalated into a yearly ceremonial celebration.

This celebration, known to the whites as the Green Corn Ceremony, was called Poskita (Posketta) or Busk by the Muscogee. Busk, meaning to fast, was observed in mid July to early August when the new corn crop ripened. Depending on the size of the town, the celebration could last from three to eight days. Being one of the larger and more important towns in the confederacy, the Busk celebration at Tuckabatchee lasted for seven or eight days. This was a much anticipated event in the life of the Muscogee people, serving as a time of thanksgiving and spiritual renewal. It also began a new year and amnesty was proclaimed, forgiving all crimes except murder.

Tribal members who had been barred from the town were allowed to return. Old clothing, pots and household utensils, furniture and food were collected and thrown away. Houses and the town square were swept and cleaned. New corn was harvested and prepared into various dishes by the women. After a time of fasting, for up to three days, all fires were extinguished. The high priest then made a new fire in the public square. This fire would burn in the council house until the next Busk and town members were supplied with a new fire for their home. The women would take the corn, as well as other food, to the town square for a grand feast. The men were assembled, all in new clothing and prepared to listen to the elders and beloved men give lengthy speeches. Much acee, the black drink, was consumed by the men during this time.

I must break away from the cultural world briefly to explain what acee was and the importance of this beverage to the Muscogee people. Acee, the black drink or tea was made by first parching and then boiling the leaves from the Yaupon holly or Ilex Vomitoria, a plant native to the Atlantic coast and Gulf coast, but not found in abundance in interior areas including Talisi and Tuckabatchee. Anthropologists believe the plant was obtained through trade initially, and then transplanted to grow along side the beans and corn. Dating back to the Mississippian period or possibly earlier, acee was essential to the indigenous people. Being used as a medicine, it was also consumed on a daily basis by men in the square and was very important in the ritualized ceremony of Busk.

Acee was treated with much respect and was considered a "mind and spirit altering substance," serving as both a stimulant and purifier. The preparation and serving was done carefully by specially selected people. Acee was drunk from a gourd or conch shell and from what I gather, from my research; it did not taste particularly good, possibly being bitter. The drink probably resembled the taste of very strong, unsweetened coffee or tea. I wonder if any other substance, honey or fruit, was ever added to give acee a better taste. The purpose was clearly not to enjoy acee, but to obtain the benefits from drinking it. This black drink produced clear thoughts, faster reaction and relief from fatigue. The white traders called it the black drink, due to the color, but Creek men referred to acee as the white drink. White foam which formed on the top when the drink was poured was the reason for the white name. Mainly, acee was associated with religious purification so very important in Creek culture. Let's return now to that cultural life of the Talisi-Tuckabatchee.

In the evening, the women were invited to the square ground where singing and dancing continued for as many as three days. All town members, as well as the children, were included in the celebration. With superstitious fear of reprisal from the Great Spirit, anyone refusing to observe the Busk was either punished or banned from the town. Friends and family from other towns would come to join in the celebration, thus forming cultural traditions.

This celebration of Busk, beginning centuries ago in the Mississippian time period, is still practiced today and is an important part of Muscogee culture — a culture that has, because of its endurance and perseverance and will of the Great Spirit — survives the test of time.

Chapter 14
Clan Social System

I briefly mentioned the Muscogee Clan System earlier and now it is a good time to talk more about the subject. The most important social structure in their lives was the clan system. Quite remarkable actually for a race of people considered primitive to have such a well organized social structure. The Muscogee were a close group of people who were matrilineal, meaning they traced their blood line through their mother. The simplest way to explain the clan system is to say they were family, just as our culture is family based today. The main difference is our culture includes the father as well.

Virtually everyone was a member of a clan; anyone not was considered an outcast and was most likely banned from the town and left to be on his own. Clan members supported and defended each other, helping and caring for those in need. This included, helping to raise children and caring for the aged and homeless, extending beyond the limits of their town. Clan membership also encompassed many from other towns in the Muscogee Nation. Clan retaliation was strictly enforced, even in the case of accidents. If a member of one clan was injured by someone from a different clan, then the males of the injured person's clan were expected to and did retaliate. This also included the elderly and the children. The only exception to this law was forgiveness during Busk.

Clan names were derived from animals and natural phenomenon. At least fifty names have been found to exist. These names included Wind, Bear, Bird, Beaver, Raccoon, Alligator, Water Moccasin, Deer and Panther, with the Wind Clan being the most powerful. All nine still exist today in Muscogee Culture. Other clans from Muscogee history which were also important included the Fish, Polecat, Fox, Potato and Red Paint Clans.

Marriage or sexual relations within a clan was supposedly forbidden, but did on rare occasions occur. This may have resulted in the offending persons being banned from the town. Clan alliance was stronger at times than allegiance to the village or town. Clan affiliation within a town, especially in early times, was based on the colors white and red, or peace and war. White was of course a peace town, while red was considered a war town. Talisi and Tuckabatchee, like all Muscogee towns, strictly adhered to the clan social system and the lifestyles of both towns were greatly influenced by their clan affiliation.

Chapter 15
Chiefs and Prophets

I wonder if people realize that neither the Muscogee nor any of the other Indian tribes had a chief as their leader. In the Mississippian time period, the headman had much authority and was considered to be nobility. The position usually was passed on to a son or relative, but by the historical period this had changed and the headman received less homage. By the 1700s, within the Native culture, no single person was in charge of the town, nor could the people be told what to do by others. The Europeans and early Americans had no concept of this leadership structure.

The word chief is actually European and was given to the Indian headman in the early contact years. Early whites singled out a person they considered as a headman creating a position of more power for him. The Creek name for this headman was miko or micco. The miko (micco) and his council of elders, which were made up of beloved wise men, governed the town.

His authority was wielded mainly by persuasion. The miko (micco) primarily dealt with civil affairs. Leading warriors, known as tustunukulgi, made most of the decisions in times of war. Tustunukee thluko or the big warrior was the most important of these men. Each town had their own miko (micco), council and a big warrior managing their affairs. It wasn't until after contact with whites, that towns were grouped together with a common "Chief."

In time of sickness the Heles-hayulgi was summoned. This was the Muscogee name for a doctor or medicine man. These men were carefully trained in the nature of diseases and the medicine used for the cure. They were very important and powerful, having the ability and responsibility for purifying and protecting the town people.

Then there were the keethla or knowers. These men had extreme spiritual power and wisdom and were thought to be able to predict death and to perform magical feats. The white traders referred to these men as prophets. These prophets would play a huge role in the upcoming Creek Civil War. Apparently, leaders in the Muscogee (Creek) society had strong consideration for the feelings of their people. With only limited power, the mikos (miccos) and prophets managed to maintain balance and harmony among their people.

Chapter 16
Ball Play

We in the deep South like football, in fact, some of us love it. Team members enjoy playing and the fans enjoy watching, each pulling for their favorite team to win. There is always much excitement on game days. It is game day, two-hundred plus years ago in our town of Tuckabatchee. The game is not football, but a game resembling modern day lacrosse, the Creeks call it "little brother of war."

Having its beginning in the Woodland time period, the game was and is today, played with extreme passion. Being more than just a game, serious plans would have been made between two neighboring towns, usually a red town and white town. In fact, practice games were often played between the different clans of a town. All males were expected to participate and eagerly anticipated playing, with many well known across the Creek Nation as great ballplayers.

The date decided, the trees and underbrush cleared and both teams were given good medicine made by the town medicine man. A dance, with women attending, had been held the previous night. Being a disgrace to sleep before a ball game, the men had not slept nor had they eaten.

The time is near. Men, women, the elderly and the children from both towns gather around the ball ground, the excitement building to a crescendo. Loud shouts can be heard from the opposing team members, concealed just out of the view of the crowd.

Then from opposite directions, they come, continuing to shout and insult the opposing players, the crowd cheering for their team. They line up in the center of the field, placing their sticks in front of them, to be counted, making sure the teams were evenly matched in number. They are dressed quite simply, wearing only breechcloths and moccasins with white or red eagle feathers in their hair, to differentiate between the teams. Some have the tails of panthers or other animals fastened around their waste, while others have painted their bodies. They appear quite fantastic to their supporters.

The signal is given, the shrill sound from a cane flute or a single beat of a drum. The referee takes the ball to the center of the field, which could range from 150 to 300 yards in length. Two upright poles stand ten feet apart on both sides of the playing field, serving as goals. The object of course, is to put the ball made of deer hide and about the size of a baseball, between the goal post. Each player wielded two sticks made from a strong hickory limb, with rawhide cup-like thongs attached to one end. The ball will be tossed from player to player and eventually reach the goal. The only rule being, no hands allowed to touch the ball. The point total of twenty goals is previously agreed on by both teams.

The crowd is ready; wagers including personal belongings have been made on the game's outcome. The team players, using extreme control, stand perfectly still. The only movement seen is the ripple of taunt muscles, flexing down their brown legs as beads of moisture form on their arms and painted faces. Before the game can begin, a speech must be given by a gifted orator, proclaiming the importance of winning and reminding the players that cheating will not be allowed. At the very moment of total eruption from both the crowd and the team players, the ball is thrown into the air and the game begins.

Dozens of nearly naked Creek warriors attempt to secure the ball, all the while running, and tackling, hitting, tripping, and doing whatever to take the ball away. Some of the players are hurt, sustaining cuts, bruises, a broken arm or leg and on occasion, but not in today's game, a player will be killed. Later, all will be forgiven and no anger will be shown. The game will continue for many hours, until one of the teams reaches the twenty point total. Today our Tuckabatchee team wins!

Team members and Tuckabatchee people are ecstatic with celebration. The opposing team and their town members dejectedly start back down-river to their village. Some, having wagered all of their personal belongings, including their clothing, will need to go home in breechcloths. To lose was an embarrassment and was a huge disappointment, but plans are already underway for a rematch on a future date.

The ball game was of tremendous importance to the Creeks and other native people. Many distinguished European and American leaders found the game very entertaining, including the Marquis de Lafayette, who watched such a game at Fort Mitchell in 1825.

In September of 1943, the *Tallassee Tribune* printed a series of articles written by the late Dr. J. M. Glenn, a Methodist minister who served in the Tallassee area in the 1930s and '40s. Dr. Glenn wrote a very accurate history of Tallassee. As far as I know, it was never published in book form. In one of his articles, he gave a very precise location for the Talisi ball ground, which is still recognizable today. Leaving Tallassee on the Lower Tuskegee Road, or the Lower River Road, as it was formerly called, continue past Stone Creek for three or four miles to the intersection of Burney Road. From this point, one can look back toward Tallassee; to the northwest, to the right side of the road in the direction of a noticeably large hill which extends for about two miles before a gentle slope downward. On the back side of the hill is the current Tallassee Airport and Babe Ruth Baseball field. It was on the flat surface of this hill that many ball games, much like the one I just described took place.

On some warm sunny day, take a leisurely ride down the Lower Tuskegee Road, turn the radio off, let the windows down, pull off to the side and listen … Its time, the ball game is just beginning. Listen closely, after two-hundred years the sounds of the ball players and their cheering fans can still be heard, for those of us who really want to hear.

Chapter 17
Talisi Royalty

In early times, women could, although rarely, achieve the position of Chieftainess, such as the Lady of Cofachiqui, whom DeSoto met in the Coosa province. Unfortunately, records of history do not show any such female power here in the Talisi-Tuckabatchee area, although I'm sure many who were considered beloved women, were very important. We do have several women with Talisi-Tuckabatchee connections who should be mentioned.

Let's begin with Coosaponakeesa, A.K.A. Mary Musgrove Bosomworth, or just simply, Creek Mary. Legend has it that Mary was the daughter of a Tuckabatchee woman and a South Carolina trader. She was born around 1700, educated in South Carolina and supposedly became a Christian. Her mother was a sister of Old Brim, known as Emperor of the Creeks, from the town of Coweta. If this is true, then Mary was the daughter of a princess. At any rate, Mary led a very important and powerful life.

She and her first husband, John Musgrove, established a trading post on the Savannah River in 1732. Securing a trade monopoly and having close ties with Georgia governor, John Oglethorpe, Mary became very wealthy, monetarily and in land ownership, which included several islands off the Georgia coast. She became a deciding factor in maintaining peace between the early Georgia colonists and the Muscogee Nation.

After Musgrove's death in 1734, Mary had two more husbands, Jacob Matthews and Thomas Bosomworth, both who enjoyed spending her previously amassed fortune. In fact, Mary and Bosomworth, in an attempt to elude creditors, retreated to Tuckabatchee in the summer of 1750.

Coosaponakeesa, Creek Mary's regal life came to an end in 1763.

After first losing and then reclaiming title to her property, the Creek princess found her final resting place on the Georgia island of St. Catherine. For anyone intrigued with the "Tuckabatchee Princess," may I recommend the fictionalized book entitled, *Creek Mary's Blood*, written by Dee Brown, a great read. The Tallassee Community Library has this book, but if you wish to own it, I suggest you go on line to a rare book site, as this book is most likely out of print. I liked it well enough to read it three or four times and maybe one day I'll read it again.

Moving on, now, to the next Talisi-Tuckabatchee royalty connection, one that is probably a little more recognizable, that of Princess Sehoy. During the early years of Fort Toulouse, Captain Marchand de Courte, Commander of the Alabama District, met and fell in love with the beautiful Sehoy of the Wind Clan. Their marriage was brief; Marchand was killed in a mutiny in 1723, but not before a daughter, Sehoy II was born.

Sehoy II first married Scotch traders, Malcomb Mcpherson and later Lachlan McGillivary. She and McGillivary had three children, Sophia, Janet and Alexander, as in Alexander McGillivary, the great Creek leader during the early years following American independence from England. In future years, Sehoy's children and grandchildren would become leaders of the Creek Nation. So, where is the Talisi-Tuckabatchee connection?

The Sehoy II saga is confusing and it did transpire a very long time ago. Some historians have Sehoy II marrying the wrong man, among other possible errors. My research shows, and it is very hard to be totally accurate, that in 1756, after deciding the Creek way of life was not for him, Lachlan McGillivary left Sehoy II and her children at Hickory Ground on the Coosa River. Being only in her mid 30s and, I imagine, still very pretty, Sehoy II was free to take another husband. Now, if my sources are correct, this is the Tuckabatchee connection. A Tuckabatchee Chief, one source has his name as Eagle Wings, had been attracted to

Sehoy II for a long time. He and Sehoy II married and like her mother before her, the marriage was of short duration. Eagle Wings was killed on a hunting trip shortly after the birth of their daughter, Sehoy III. The haunting story of Sehoy III is long and one that has very little to do with Tuckabatchee. She had a child by a Jacob Monaic, and later entered into a prearranged marriage with a man by the name of John Tate. Sehoy III and Tate had a son, David, who figured prominently in the Creek War, on the side of the whites. After Tate's death, Sehoy III married a Scotsman, Charles Weatherford. They had a son, William. Most people with only the vaguest knowledge of Alabama history are familiar with William, the Red Eagle.

Our story is not that of Red Eagle, although I will return to him later, nor is it one at length of the Sehoy's, but it is of importance to mention their connections to Tuckabatchee.

Several people presently living in the Tallassee area have done extensive genealogical research and have found definite proof of being descendants of the Sehoys or Red Eagle. I have both Cherokee and Creek ancestry, but to be a descendant of the Sehoys is really special. I know one particular lady, a proven descendant, who when compared to Sehoy I's portrait, actually resembles Sehoy I. That's awesome! As with Creek Mary, I am fascinated by the three Sehoys and their story, but it is time to move on.

Chapter 18
The Traders

As mentioned, the first documented traders did not arrive in the Talisi-Tuckabatchee area until around 1686. The earliest trade items of colored beads and trinkets probably delighted the women and children, and the useful items, the axe and hoe really made an impression with the men. The native people knew right away that these items and others like them could make their lives easier. That it did. Tuckabatchee, being a large and important town, attracted more and more traders. There were governmental regulations later on, but in the early years traders flocked to the town. Many found the Creek women to be very pretty and also industrious, as they were accustomed to doing hard work. The traders were far from home and lonely, thus unions were formed. Some of these unions did include marriages in a Creek ceremony. Of course, children would come and this would be the beginning of generations of people with Native American blood, which continues today.

Some of the traders would leave their trade goods and maybe their child and then move on, while others would stay. Usually, these were the ones who did marry and were willing to change their lifestyle to that of the Creeks. These men were known as Indian Countrymen and many often became wealthy and influential, their children and grandchildren would be some of the future leaders of the Creek Nation. The identity of most traders was not recorded or was lost over time. Many who came to the Talisi-Tuckabatchee area were good men and many would stay to become productive. One such trader was a Mr. Walker, who came to Tuckabatchee in the early 1800s. He would marry a daughter of Civil Chief Big Warrior and become prosperous and influential. His descendants still live in the Tallassee area today.

In order to enter into the trade agreements, the Creek men must have had something to trade. After all, the traders did want something in return, and they were not very interested in the pottery bowls or the finely crafted arrows manufactured by the Creeks. They wanted the skins of the deer and other animals that were abundant in the area. This would begin a sequence of events that would over the next two centuries turn the tide for native people, not only at Talisi and Tuckabatchee, but the entire country.

Books have been written regarding the trade system and its effect on the native people, but I think I can simply and briefly explain it here. In the beginning trade goods were a luxury. It wasn't long before the goods were a necessity and the Creeks became dependent upon them. Creek men would spend months at a time on the hunt, trying to satisfy the demands of the traders and their own need for the trader's goods. This practice would continue for about one-hundred years, until there were no more deer.

The trader set up a store or factory, as it was called. Here the Creek men would bring the deer pelts to trade for the wares of the white man, including whiskey or fire water. This was another evil for the Creeks that would contribute to their undoing. Of course, many of the traders would purposely cheat the Creek men in the trade, giving them far less than the value of their skins. Some traders would even go as far as to fix the scales, so the weight would not be accurate. The Creek men were of course aware of this, but because of their need to have the trade goods and the fire water, they allowed the unjust treatment to continue.

Hundreds of thousands of deer pelts were shipped to Europe during this time period. In fact, my late father-in-law, who was born in 1917, stated, when he was a boy, there were virtually no deer in the Tallassee area. What took a century to deplete would take another century to replenish.

During the time period between the late 1600s and the late 1700s, political power would not come from European countries, but within the Colonies and later the new country of America. Very few deer remained, which was of no importance to the Americans who did not want deer, they could hunt their own. They wanted something of much more importance. From the outset, the Americans wanted the homes of the deer and also that of the native people, they wanted the land.

Some things really never change, especially when it has to do with desiring the unaffordable. Today, most people have the easily attained credit card. Need something? Want something? Just charge it! That's good as long as payment can be made, but sometimes this can create trouble. The Creeks, of course, did not have credit cards, but they did have a similar problem. After the decline of the deer and the emergence of the new country, the trade goods and fire water were still desired. The Creeks would charge and charge some more, soon running up an enormous debt, which they could not pay. This was well planned. The government owned factory would just take their land for payment. This all began with the colorful beads and metal axe. The sun was, even then, beginning to set for the Creek Nation.

Chapter 19
Visitors, Those Who Came and Those Who Stayed

Due to the importance, the location and the beauty of the Tallapoosa River Valley, many famous and influential people came to visit and stay in Talisi and Tuckabatchee. One such person was James McQueen, who was thought to have been the first white man to make permanent residence in Talisi. McQueen came here in 1733, after serving as a soldier under Governor Oglethorpe in Georgia. Some historical stories tell that he first settled in the Talladega, Alabama area among the Natchez and later moved, along with some of the Natchez to Talisi. McQueen became a planter and was very powerful and influential with the Talisi people. He married a Talisi woman and had a very large family of mixed breeds. Living to be 128 years old, he was said to be related in some way to almost everyone in the town. His son Peter became a redstick war leader in the Creek War of 1813-14. Another descendent was a great grandson, Billy Powell, son of William and Polly. Billy was born in 1805, on Casta Bogah Creek, in a village which was a branch of Talisi east of the main town. Many erroneously believe that Billy was born in Talisi, when actually the site is closer to Tuskegee. He and his mother migrated to Florida after the Creek War. The name Billy Powell may not be recognizable, but I would imagine the name Osceola is. Billy Powell would be known in future years as Osceola, the great Seminole War leader. I wonder how many people living in Tallassee today can trace their ancestry back to James and Peter or maybe even Osceola? I'm sure there are those who can.

Another visitor who came to Talisi in the summer of 1776, was William Bartram. Bartram was a Philadelphia botanist who traveled over the southern parts of the country collecting plant specimens. His manuscripts, since published in book form, offer excellent detail of daily life of the Creeks during this time period. I would recommend this book entitled, Travels of William Bartram, edited by Mark Van Doren, a good source for anyone wishing to expand their knowledge of Creek life. Bartram spent time in the Talisi area on two separate occasions. He was very much impressed with Talisi and the upriver site of the falls. He stated that this would make a wonderful American city. I believe he definitely called that one right.

Countless other important people, both European and American, as well as native leaders from other tribes, converged on the town of Tuckabatchee. Many, many treaties would be haggled over and signed here. Of course, by this time period, the most important commodity to the whites and to the Creeks was the ground they walked on, Mother Earth, the land. Many would come to try to separate the Creeks from their homeland.

One of, if not, the most important people to come was Benjamin Hawkins. Hawkins arrived in Tuckabatchee in 1796, as a United States Indian Agent. While he made his home on the Flint River in the eastern portion of the Creek Confederacy; he would spend much time during the next twenty years, here on the Tallapoosa.

Like Bartram, Hawkins found Tuckabatchee to be a beautiful place. He too saw great potential in the upriver falls to be utilized for water power and the giant gray boulders which could be used for the construction of buildings. From the very beginning, he saw Tuckabatchee and the surrounding area, not as a peaceful native village, but as a great WHITE American city. The United States government sent Benjamin Hawkins south, in particular to Tuckabatchee; to teach the townspeople how to become better farmers, to use the plow and the loom. Hawkins also influenced the Creeks to wear the white man clothing, to speak his English, to worship his God — and to become civilized.

Hawkins did become fond of the Tuckabatchee people and many became his friends and close confidants, but after all, he did have a job to do, and he did it well. The United States government had sent him not to improve the lives of the Creeks, but to change their lifestyle, to teach them to live as whites. There was an ulterior motive, the land. The Americans wanted it and would have it at any cost to the native people. Benjamin Hawkins became a major figure in treaty negotiations and in my opinion was very instrumental in creating the division in Creek society, which would lead to the Creek Civil War.

Concave indention where a stone bowl was cut from the soapstone quarry at Coon Creek

Debra Hughey and niece Jalee King show a stone bowl that was formed but never cut from the soapstone quarry at Coon Creek.

Large Woodland or early Mississippian period mound at Tuckabatchee.

Debra Hughey shows glass trade bead found at Talisi village site known locally as "Townhouse Hill."

Debra Hughey examines pottery sherds scattered over a cotton field that was once the village of Tuckabatchee.

Dovard Taunton's 1984 painting of two Native Americans spearing stripped bass on the rocks of the Tallapoosa River.

UPPER AND LOWER CREEK TOWNS

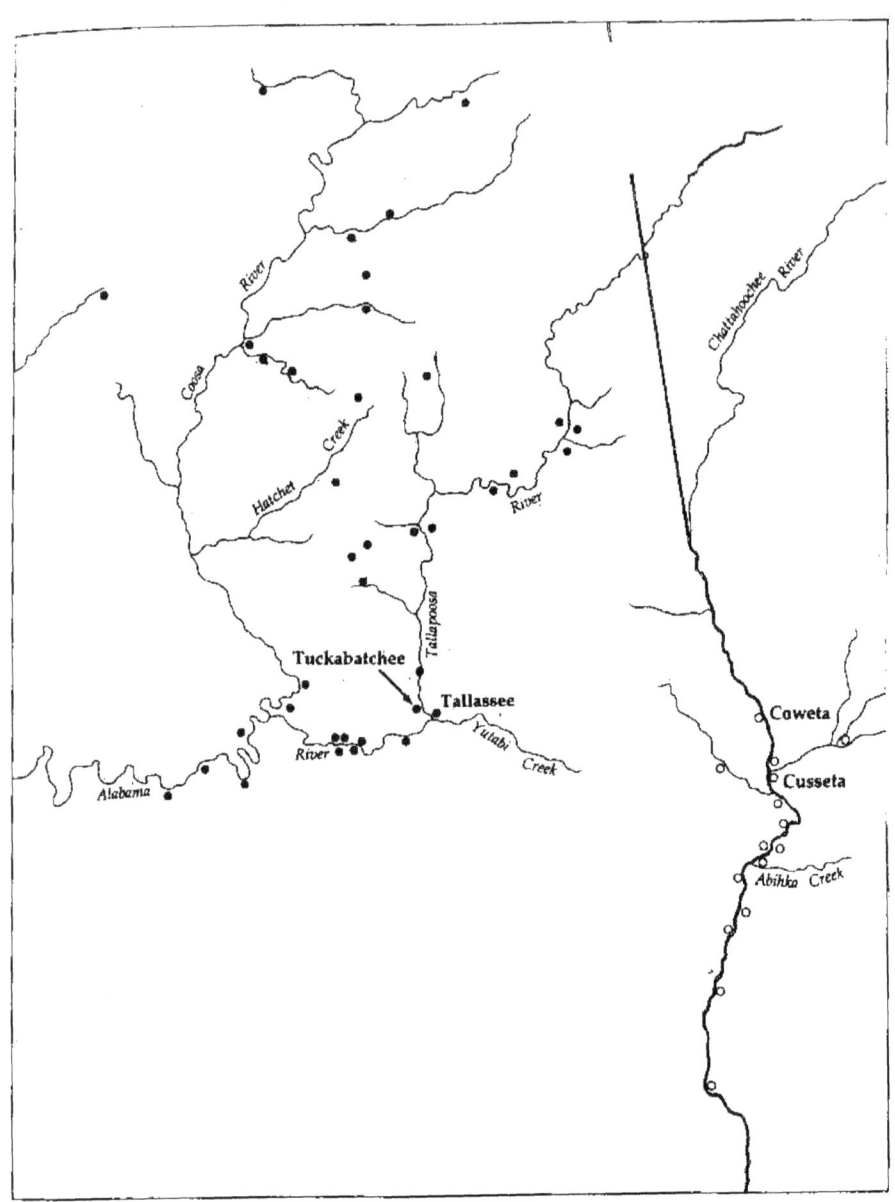

Creek Village Sites in Alabama, circa 1800.

1790 portrait of Talisi Chief Hopoithle Mico.

Chief Big Warrior of Tuckabatchee.

1790 Portrait of Talisi Chief Opothle Yoholo.

1838 George Catlin portrait of Osceola who was a Talisi Creek born between the present-day towns of Tallassee and Tuskegee, Alabama.

According to Thomas Woodward, Osceola was born near where the Western Railroad of Alabama crosses Eufaupee Creek. The author stands at or very near that site which is located in present-day Macon County, Alabama.

The William Weatherford "Red Eagle" grave site in northern Baldwin County, Alabama.

Historical Marker at site of Fort Mims in Baldwin County, Alabama.

Randall Hughey with ancient "Stick Ball" field at Fort Mitchell, Alabama in the background.

The Great Council Oak at Tuckabatchee, circa 1921-29. Property owner George Lamberth poses along with his 1926 Chevrolet.

An undated sketch of Forts Decatur and Borroughs located on the south boundary of Tuckabatchee.

84 Debra Hughey

Earthworks at the site of Fort Burroughs.

Monument at Fort Decatur.

The Creek "Trail of Tears" historical marker at Fort Mitchell, Alabama.

One of several bronze plaques at Fort Mitchell, Alabama, with hundreds of names of Creeks Indians, including many from Talisi/Tuckabatchee who were removed via boat down the Chattahoochee River and eventually to Indian Territory in Arkansas and Oklahoma.

Thurlow Dam was built in the early 1930s at the site of the "Great Falls" in Tallassee, Alabama.

Modern-day Muscogee perform an ancient ceremony on Tallapoosa River in June of 2010.

The Tallapoosa River

Chapter 20
Cultural Breakdown

By the early years of the 19th century, with the help of Hawkins and others like him, drastic changes had taken place within Creek culture. The pleasures of the white man's trade items had adversely changed their lives. For more than a century, many Creeks were slowly becoming acculturated. During that century, many children had been born whose fathers were Scottish, Irish, British and other nationalities. Creek blood was no longer pure. Even the mixture of the different native tribes that formed the great Muscogee Confederacy would become a factor in the cultural disintegration.

The Creek people had changed. They were no longer the simple people whose main goal was survival. Many had become wealthy and powerful by Creek standards. More often than not, it was the half breeds who welded the power. A caste social system of sorts had developed and a slight rift was created. The towns were no longer closely knit, in fact, by the early 1800s many of the Talisi people had re-settled for some twenty miles up Euphaupee Creek. The town of Tuckabatchee extended for three miles or so along the west bank of the Tallapoosa River, with many of the residents being of a different moiety. The best way to define the word moiety, in today's terms, would be sort of like comparing Republicans and Democrats, liberal and conservative and yes, the middle as well. Because of these moieties, there was a difference of opinion about many things. Much has been written about the Creek cultural division, and what would seem simple, is actually a complicated issue. In reading about this, I have tried to put the various opinions and factors together to come up with some definite pattern of opinions and ideas, but I do not think there was one other than a scene of a fractured society.

One influencing factor would be that of blood lines, the Muscogee and other native groups and those mixed with European and finally White Americans. Creek interaction with white people, and exposure to their customs and culture would have certainly been most impressionable.

This interaction increased the wealth among the more progressive of the Creeks. Some of the Creeks patterned their lifestyle after that of whites, while others remained totally native. Those with more white blood became the most progressive. Now, here is the strange part, the wealthy, progressive Creeks would be the ones in the near future, who became the leaders in the Creek War against the whites. This division and period of unrest within the Talisi and Tuckabatchee people and the entire Creek Confederacy would continue to escalate for the next several years.

Chapter 21
The Shooting Star

By late summer, in the year 1811, the stage was set for the arrival of a visitor from the north with Tuckabatchee ties. He called himself a man of the Tallapoosa. He was the shooting star, he was Tecumseh. The events that would transpire after his arrival would forever change Creek culture.

The Shawnee had lived among the Creeks during the late 17th and early 18th centuries, and may have, in fact, helped to settle the town of Tuckabatchee. Some historians say that Puckshinwah, the father of Tecumseh, was a Shawnee born on the Tallapoosa, while others think he was part Creek. Still others argue that Methotasa, (A Turtle Laying Her Eggs In The Sand), Tecumseh's mother, was of Creek/Shawnee descent or perhaps a full blood Creek. Confusing isn't it? Read five books about Tecumseh and get four different versions of his blood line. We do know that his family was here and one or the other, or perhaps both of his parents had Creek blood. I believe I will settle with the mother.

Tecumseh's parents remained here until about 1760, before returning north to Ohio. In March of 1768, underneath the brilliance of a streaking meteor, the Shooting Star, Tecumseh was born. From the book, *A Sorrow In Our Heart*, by Allan W. Eckert, he states that the Shooting Star was an older sister of Tecumseh and he was actually known as The Panther Passing Across or Panther In The Sky. Regardless of what he was called, this brilliant light streaking across the sky was a great omen of what the baby boy would become.

Intelligent and always a leader as a child, Tecumseh became one of the most respected and possibly the most well known Native American of his time. He became an adult during the dawn of America and experienced first hand the struggle and hardship dealt to the native people by first the British and then the Americans. Tecumseh had great foresight of the future for his people and realized that without an alliance of ALL Indians there would be little hope of survival.

This hope of alliance was the purpose for this trip back to the former homeland of his parents. Actually he came twice, a couple years prior, and then the all important trip in the late summer of 1811. Tecumseh left Ohio in August along with his entourage of Shawnee, Kickapoo, Creek, one of which was Seekaboo, who had Tuckabatchee ties, and also braves from other unknown tribes.

Tecumseh stopped at various villages along the way. Most had already pledged their support to the great leader. Upon entering the south however, he must have been more than a little surprised to find different opinions and even open opposition to his Pan-Indian plan of uniting tribes to oppose white culture and intrusion. The Chickasaw listened politely to what he had to say, but refused to commit. The Choctaw, under the leadership of powerful chief Pushmataha, were defiant, harsh and insulting and called Tecumseh a trouble maker. Extremely disappointed, he would leave the Choctaw, only to be followed for several days by Pushmataha and his warriors. The Choctaw chief would not allow Tecumseh to speak, even to those wanting to hear his message.

Moving on toward the south and east, a delegation of Cherokee visited the camp of Tecumseh. Having planned to visit the country of the Cherokee later, he was pleased to see them, until he received a message from their chief. Tecumseh was told that the Cherokee were at peace with the white Americans and had no plans to unite with him, in fact, if he came to their country, he would be killed.

What must have Tecumseh's reaction been to this disturbing revelation? The great leader of the Shawnee must have been humiliated, embarrassed, angered and above all, deeply saddened. Tecumseh knew he had to have the cooperation and help from all the tribes if his hope for the survival of native culture was to continue. He knew the intent of both the British and the Americans and he knew his red brothers of the south had been deceived, but all was not lost, not yet. He was still to visit the land of his parents, the land of the Creeks. Were they not the bravest and most ferocious of all the southern tribes? Were they not his family? They would be open to his message and unite with him. These must have been his thoughts as he and his group of dedicated warriors headed into the Confederacy of the mighty Creek Nation.

Chapter 22
Tecumseh on the Tallapoosa

At Tuckabatchee on the River Tallapoosa, in September 1811, thousands of people, Creek, Cherokee, and Choctaw, American officials, traders and scouts converged on the town for the Grand National Council. Agent Benjamin Hawkins was present; his agenda was to tell the Creeks about the new road, the Federal Road, which would soon be built through the center of their nation. This, of course, was met with opposition from the Creeks, who knew to grant the government permission to build a road, would be like opening a door for the influx of white settlers. Hawkins won and the Creeks were right. Over the next several years, many thousand white families from Virginia and North Carolina traveled over the Federal Road to make their homes near and sometimes inside the Creek Nation.

These important council activities had been going on for several days, but the main reason for the huge attendance, especially the visitors from other tribes, was the much anticipated appearance of the Shawnee leader. While most were excited about his visit, there were some, one in particular, who was not pleased, Tastanagi Tako, Big Warrior, the head civil chief of Tuckabatchee. As speaker for all the Upper Creeks, he was the most important leader on the National Council. Quite impressive in appearance, Big Warrior was a large man in statue and was reported to have been as spotted as a leopard. Possibly, not a full blood Creek, some historians think he too had the blood of the northern tribes. Big Warrior was cunning and a little deceitful, but also intelligent. He did not like Benjamin Hawkins and cared even less for the white government, seeing through their so-called benevolence to help the red race. Pretending friendship, Big Warrior hid his true feelings regarding the whites. Having plans to unite the southern tribes under his own leadership, Big

Warrior was resentful and jealous of the Shawnee leader and his ideas for a Pan-Indian society.

This mattered very little on the evening of September 19th, as Tecumseh and his group of followers arrived at the public square where the council house was located. Historical sources and local legend place this as the site of the great Tuckabatchee Council Oak. Let us pause briefly in the account of Tecumseh's grand entrance to give some intriguing and probably unknown information regarding the Council Oak.

Thomas Woodward states the Oak was located in front of the house of half breed Sukey Cornells. The tree was "held as sacred," and was a meeting place in the early 1800s for the Indians. The tree may have played a part in the early founding of Tuckabatchee and was considered a landmark before removal of the Creeks.

The large oak was damaged by storms in 1909 and again in 1920 and in 1922, suffered damage from a fire, but still remained standing in 1929. There are pictures showing the remnants of the sad forlorn tree where so much history had taken place. The Alabama Department of Archives and History has a manuscript sketch map of the tree.

Dr. Knight in his study of Tuckabatchee accurately located the site of the old oak, where in 1929 a dedication marker had been placed. The marker which read: "This Stone Placed at the Great Council Tree Marks the Site of Tuckabatchee, 1686-1836," had been pushed into the river by military contractors during World War II. Fortunately, the marker was found and is currently located at Tallassee City Hall.

In the early 1980s, many years after the original tree had died, and only the oldest residents of Tallassee remembered where the tree stood, a new sapling was planted. Today it has grown into a pretty tree, but there is nothing there to indicate its significance except for an old chain link fence encircling it. The replaced tree is located just beyond the GKN industrial property fence line on Alabama Highway 229 south of Tallassee.

Now for the intriguing part, of which most people are unaware. Historical and archaeological evidence show the Tuckabatchee square ground was much further down river than the current Council Oak site. The tree was supposed to have been near the square ground. Oops! Also, Woodward — and he was there — said the original tree had been cut down by a tenant farmer, while he owned the property in the early nineteenth century.

According to Dr Knight, the tree was old and probably dated back to 1836, but was not the Council Oak beneath which Tecumseh delivered his powerful speech.

Now let us resume. We are once again at the council beneath the branches of a magnificent oak tree that was indeed the Tuckabatchee Council Oak.

As with most major events in long ago history, there is more than one version or description of the account of Tecumseh's visit. In the book, *Tecumseh a Life*, by John Sugden, a very vivid account is given of the fantastic dress of the northern visitors. "Stripped to breech cloths, moccasins, and ornaments, they had placed eagle feathers on their heads and painted their faces black, while buffalo tails hung behind from their belts. Other tails were attached to their arms, ingeniously made to stand out, by means of bands." Sugden further states that Tecumseh and his group, the number and tribal origin again differ with various accounts "… walked several times around the square and approached the Creek chiefs with greetings and presenting them with tobacco and a show of goodwill."

Another writer describes the group as being dressed in buckskins, hunting shirts and leggings with silver bands on their arms, their faces painted black and red. I suppose, either description could be accurate, but I like the former. In September, on the Tallapoosa, buckskin clothing would have been extremely hot and uncomfortable.

Sam Dale described the group as being the most athletic body of men he had ever seen. He described Tecumseh as being about six feet tall, having an austere countenance and an imperial manner, but walked with a slight limp.

Imagine being one of the onlookers, in the midst of the excitement, seeing the great Shawnee leader and wondering what his next action would be. The occasion must have been an event all that was present would never forget and would pass on to generation after generation. Perhaps that is why there are so many different versions of his visit.

However many things occurred which appear to be consistent. One being — I'm sure to everyone's disappointment — was the fact that Tecumseh refused to give his talk on the first day he came to the council square. "The sun has gone too far down," was his reply when asked why he would not speak. A different excuse would be given each day for the next ten days. The reason for this delay was intentional. Tecumseh was waiting for Hawkins and possibly others to leave, as some historians say no whites were present on the day of the speech.

While Tecumseh stalled, Seekaboo, the mixed blood guide taught the Creeks the Dance of the Lakes. This was the war dance of the northern tribes and the Creeks learned this with great enthusiasm. Seekaboo was part Creek and had lived among the Shawnee for about twenty years. Some have said his mother lived at Tuckabatchee and that he was also related to Tecumseh. I wonder if the trip was a reunion for Seekaboo and his family. He was one of Tecumseh's strongest and most important supporters, being fluent in the Muscogee and Choctaw languages; he also served as an interpreter. Seekaboo was totally entrenched in the Pan-Indian movement and was associated with the teaching of Tecumseh's bother, Tenskwatwa, or The Prophet.

Tenskwatwa proclaimed to be a medium of the Great Spirit and had great religious influence on the Shawnee and the northern tribes.

This influence was largely responsible for the Pan-Indian reform movement which grew to a religious frenzy in parts of the country, including Tuckabatchee. The Prophet tutored his brother on this reform and Tecumseh, being much more dynamic and forceful, became the voice of The Prophet. Tecumseh emphatically believed in the benevolence of the Great Spirit and the powers He bestowed. Tecumseh continued to play the waiting game with Hawkins, but his time would come when he would relay to his people, the will of the Great Spirit, the will to preserve the Creek Nation.

Chapter 23
The Speech

After ten days had passed, Hawkins decided he would leave Tuckabatchee. He had had enough of Tecumseh's waiting game and Hawkins believed the town people were under his control and would pay little attention to what the Shawnee had to say. This may have been the time other whites either left or were asked to leave, as many sources state, no whites were present for the speech. One possible exception was Sam Dale, but at least one historian thinks he was not there either. Dale, a scout and trader spent much time among the Creeks and likely was considered a friend. He was also fluent in the Muscogee language and after the translation of Tecumseh's speech was able to understand the forceful words spoken. The words were, of course, spoken in Shawnee and then translated into Muscogee by Seekaboo. There was no written record of the heartfelt speech. Considering the fact that, the speech had to be translated and Dale's claim, even after many years, to remember verbatim every word, one would have to wonder how accurate his account was.

The powerful speech given by Tecumseh on the banks of the Tallapoosa River was one of the most important ever given by a Native American orator. From all accounts, the date was September 30, 1811, precisely at noon. Dale again gives a vivid description of the attire and actions which occurred just prior to the speech. It is my opinion he was there, if not, Dale must have had a wonderful imagination and was not being truthful.

Dale describes the group of Native Americans as being naked, except for their loin flaps and being adorned with black paint. Having angry scowls on their faces, they looked to Dale like "a procession of devils." He said Tecumseh, walking with a limp, led the warriors around the square ground. Pausing at each right angle he sprinkled the earth with tobacco and sumac. Repeating this three times, the participants approached the staff or flag pole in the center of the square. After pouring the remaining tobacco and sumac into the ceremonial fire, the group went to the council house where Big Warrior and other principle chiefs sat.

Tecumseh gave a war whoop, his followers doing the same, a wampum belt was given to Big Warrior and a Shawnee pipe was passed among the Creek chiefs. Dale describes the scene as being strange, with no words spoken. "Every thing was still as death, even the winds slept, and there was only the gentle rustle of the falling leaves."

Thousands of Indian eyes were focused on the Shawnee, each brave waiting with bated breath and eager anticipation. Looking at his audience with defiance, Tecumseh slowly began to speak. Dale said he "burned with a super natural luster, and his whole frame shook with emotion." Again, quoting Sam Dale, this is a small excerpt of the speech, which lasted for several hours.

"Let the white race perish. They seize your land; they corrupt your women; they trample on the ashes of your dead! Back, whence they came, upon a trail of blood, they must be driven. Back! Back, ay, into the great water whose accursed waves brought them to our shores! Burn their dwellings! Destroy their stock! Slay their wives and children! The Red man owns the country, and the Palefaces must never enjoy it. War now!

War forever! War upon the living! War upon the dead!"

Chapter 24
Response and Final Words

While we will never know for certain what was actually said on that day in September of 1811, I believe the account from Dale was greatly exaggerated. Tecumseh had not threatened the lives of women and children in any previous speech, so why would he do so in the homeland of his family. His underlying motive most likely was war on the whites, when the time was right. The objective of his trip south was to unite the different tribes and return them to a simpler life in preparation for the fight.

We know the words from the great Shawnee leader were strong and powerful, exciting the normally stoic braves who were ready to carry the red stick of war. Surely, his family connection with Tuckabatchee was expressed, as he invited them to join with him in the stand against the whites who desired the lands of the red man. Tecumseh would have depended on the benevolence of the Great Spirit, the Master of Breath and the love for his red children.

Big Warrior got as excited as the braves, but kept his composure, not revealing his true feelings. Remember, he had some plans of his own and I also believe he did not have the courage to fight the whites. He told the Shawnee leader that the people of Tuckabatchee were at peace with their white friends and would not join with him.

The Ridge, representing the Cherokee would also decline the invitation to join with Tecumseh. Had he foreseen the future, I imagine this decision would have been different.

In native culture during this time period, the chief did not have the power to speak for individuals. While Big Warrior and The Ridge may have been opposed to the plan of Tecumseh, many quickly rallied behind the Shawnee leader.

The Talisi's, across the river neighbors of the Tuckabatchee's, were on the other hand, eager to take up the red stick. Under the leadership of civil chief Hopoithle Mico, the Talisi King, also known as the Tame King, great animosity arose between the two towns. The aging Talisi King and Big Warrior were bitter rivals. It seems both desired the position of head of the national council. Big Warrior would achieve the title, but perhaps the title was not attained honestly.

While many other important leaders were in attendance that day, the opinion of William Weatherford, the Red Eagle, certainly should be noted. Persons with only a casual interest in Alabama history will probably be surprised to know — from at least two different accounts — Red Eagle was opposed to the plans of Tecumseh. He said to join with him would be the wrong choice to make and the Creeks should remain neutral because the whites were many and strong. In the course of the next two years, Red Eagle's opinion changed and for a good reason. More on that change later.

After the attending chiefs had all been given the opportunity to express their feelings, either in opposition or in agreement with Tecumseh, he would have the final word. He again spoke of the Great Spirit. Tecumseh told the people of Tuckabatchee that a great light, an arm of fire would stretch across the sky over Tuckabatchee. This would be a sign from the Great Spirit.

Soon after the prophesy, the village people watched in awe as night after night the predicted light filled the skies and shone eerily over the town. I imagine the light in the sky may have changed the mind-set of many, since the Creeks were a superstitious people, believing in signs from the Great Spirit.

The light became brighter during the month of October and slowly vanished by November. This must have been quite impressive as the head of the light, which was in fact a comet, stretched a million miles across, with the tail extending one hundred million miles long. Filling the entire sky, night must have appeared as bright as day. No wonder the Creeks believed this was a sign; had I been there, I would have too.

Tecumseh did not reveal that he knew in advance of the comet. His British astronomer friends had told him of its appearance in Europe earlier in the year and that it would streak southern skies in the fall.

Tecumseh and his group of followers remained among the Creeks for a month, visiting other towns. He continued to incite and recruit, gaining more support for his cause. The bright light that continued to illuminate the night skies undoubtedly reminded the Creeks of the powerful words of the great leader.

Before leaving, Tecumseh had a final statement for Big Warrior. Pointing his finger at the large man, who had refused to join with him, the Shawnee leader is reported to have said, "your blood is white…you do not believe the Great Spirit has sent me. You shall believe it. I will leave directly and go straight to Detroit. When I get there, I will stamp my foot upon the ground and shake down every house in Tuckabatchee."

Tecumseh then left Tuckabatchee and the Creek Confederacy. Seekaboo would stay, continuing to acquire more support, while some of the Creeks went north with Tecumseh.

On the 16th of December, 1811, the people of Tuckabatchee were awakened from their sleep as the ground beneath them began to shake and houses began to fall. Even in their fright, the people knew Tecumseh had arrived back home, he had stomped his foot and just as he had predicted, the houses fell.

Of course, we now know the violent shaking of the earth was caused by the New Madrid earthquake, one of the strongest to ever rock this country. The tremors were experienced from Missouri to the east coast and they were also felt in Tuckabatchee. The series of shocks continued until February.

Tecumseh may have known about the appearance of the comet in 1811, but there is absolutely no way he could have known about an earthquake. Is it possible that the Great Spirit could have had something to do with the shaking of the earth? Probably not, but the Creeks sure thought so.

****

The eastern portion of the United States rarely experiences the power of an earthquake. Strangely enough, in 2011, one day after I wrote this story of Tecumseh's quake, moderately strong tremors shook Virginia and Washington, D.C., just days before the 200th anniversary of the tremor that rocked Tuckabatchee. One never knows …

****

Now here is a final note regarding the renowned Shawnee leader, Tecumseh. He continued to travel the country, visiting other native towns. Many joined with him in his effort to preserve the Indian culture, while others scorned and ridiculed him. He did not see the plan to unify his people become a reality nor did he see the consequences of their failure to do so.

The valiant Tecumseh died in battle on the Tames River in Canada in October of 1813. The night prior to the battle, he predicted his own death, just as he had predicted the ground would shake two years earlier.

Chapter 25
After the Shooting Star

The visit of Tecumseh and the events which occurred during and after his stay at Tuckabatchee certainly influenced the opinions and ideals of the people. After finding the town in a state of unrest and discord, Tecumseh and Seekaboo further increased hostility, provided a plan of action and most significantly, proved the evidence of supernatural support. The nativist faction, or those wishing to retain native ways, continued to increase as the mood, not only in Tuckabatchee, but the entire Creek Confederacy grew tense and dark.

Again, there was not a clear pattern for division. Some full-bloods felt strongly about maintaining the Creek culture and agreed completely with Tecumseh's ideals. On the other hand there was one group of metizos, half Creek and half white, who preferred a white life style. Then lastly, there was the group of metizos who had profited most by being a mixture of Creek and white.

They were the children of traders or Indian countrymen, some having lived among the whites and having been educated in white schools. These men had obtained wealth and power, often becoming headmen or chiefs.

Not unlike the War Between the States, which would take place in fifty short years, members of the same village and even within the same family, or clan, would differ in their beliefs, some siding with the "Red Sticks" those ready to fight and die to save their land, and others taking the side of the white or peace faction.

Another definite factor in the increasing unrest in the Creek Confederacy was the little horse path which was now called the Federal Road. Remember, this was a major topic during the grand council, with Hawkins informing the Tuckabatchee that the road was going to be enlarged, like it or not. Hundreds of white families would continue down this road, greatly increasing the white population near the Creek boundaries. These land-hungry setters, who were just passing through, had no problem building their log cabins on Creek land, if they could get away with it. It was acceptable to deal with traders and the occasional white man who wanted to live as they did, but entire families who came encroaching on their land was a different matter entirely.

This was how the final chapters of the Creek saga began. After thousands of years of cultural progression, their association with the whites and the problems it created caused the rift within Creek society which hastened the destruction of their culture.

The Creek Civil War of 1812-1813, not only changed the lives of the Creek people, but helped to shape the future of America. Dozens of books relating to this sad story have been written, many at great length. I am going to try to briefly give the Talisi, Tuckabatchee connections to the War.

Chapter 26
Rumbles of War

Let's set the stage: Tuckabatchee, being the capital of the Creek Confederacy, was an important town. Many meetings of the council were held here and war-related activities were planned, but these plans may not be what one would think. Keep in mind, the towns and villages were classified as red, indicating war towns or white, the color signifying peace. Tuckabatchee, under the leadership of Big Warrior was considered a white town. Big Warrior had refused the red war club offered by Tecumseh, not so much because he sided with Benjamin Hawkins and the whites, but for reasons that are unclear. I have never read of Big Warrior being called a coward, but I do think he did not want to fight.

Now, across the river, the town of Talisi was literally crawling with red sticks, their leaders and prophets. The Talisi King and Big Warrior were more than just rivals, now they were on opposing sides and both would suffer the consequences.

The entire Creek Confederacy was a boiling pot of unrest, with little incidents occurring here and there between the Creeks themselves as well as with the white settlers. One such incident which may have actually provoked the start of all-out war was the murder of a former Georgia legislator. This happened in May of 1812, when a branch of Talisi's killed William Lott near Warrior Stand in present day Macon County. The motive for the murder has been forgotten or possibly never recorded. It could have been, Lott and the Talisis had some sort of disagreement, maybe a cow had been stolen after wondering on to Creek land, or maybe there was not a reason at all.

With Hawkins insistence, the Creek Council decided punishment was necessary for the action. Hawkins then sent warriors from the lower

Creek towns of Coweta and Cusseta, as well as some from Tuckabatchee, in search of the accused Talisi warriors. They were found on Notasulga Creek, a stream of which I am unfamiliar. The leader was shot, while the others returned to their town. This enraged the Talisi and Red Sticks even more. It seemed that punishment was being meted out by the Creeks own people. This is a good example of the split which continued to widen within the Creek Confederacy.

One such incident led to others, and the word was soon out, the Creeks were at war. This was not exactly true in the beginning, but as more clashes occurred, the rumor became a fact. The Creeks were at war and the above incident, involving Talisi warriors was likely the first engagement of the Creek Civil War.

Chapter 27
The Siege

The information that the Red Sticks were at war sent shock waves of fear throughout the region both in white settlements bordering the Creek Nation and also within the nation itself. The Upper Creek towns, those on the Coosa and Tallapoosa Rivers, were the main hot beds for Red Stick activity. With neighboring towns being war or peace towns, warriors wore red or white feathers in their hair to signify their alliance. The town of Autossee, just down river from Tuckabatchee was a very red town as we will see a little later.

Another incident occurred on the Duck River in the Tennessee frontier where several whites were killed. Some warriors involved in the incident were from Tuckabatchee, including Little Warrior who some sources say was the son of Big Warrior, another example of a different allegiance within a town and even a family. Also included was a Coosawa chief by the name of Captain Issacs. Punishment was again ordered and administered. The Creek Council passed a decree of death for Little Warrior. William McIntosh, of the Lower Creek town of Coweta, was sent to take care of the business. Of the accused group, five were killed at Red Warriors Bluff on the Tallapoosa. This may have been located near present day Alexander City. In a strange turn of events, Captain Issacs, who was the son-in-law of Alexander McGillivary, was sent in pursuit of the others who were not killed, initially. Little Warrior and two others were captured and killed near Wetumpka by Captain Issacs, who had apparently testified against Little Warrior for immunity from his part in the Duck River killings.

Captain Issacs, for his own reasons, like Big Warrior, had not joined with Tecumseh. He was jealous of the Shawnee and considered himself to be an important prophet. He became such a fanatic, his own followers turned against him and threatened to kill him. For some vague reason, possibly for his own protection, Captain Issacs went to Tuckabatchee, promising the white town powder, lead and reinforcements. The Red Sticks, who were referred to as hostiles, considered him to be a witch and sent word they were coming after him, but the Captain was not the only one the Red Sticks sought.

In late June of 1813, one-hundred, ninety friendly chiefs and warriors had gathered at Tuckabatchee. The town was most likely fortified at that time and must have been considered a safe place. Word had been sent to the Cherokees for assistance, but the northern neighbors did not respond.

By July, the old chiefs were alarmed and even terrified. They had received messages that the Red Sticks planned not only to attack but to destroy Tuckabatchee. True to their word, the Red Sticks came. After asking for the surrender of Big Warrior, Captain Issacs and others, which of course did not happen, the attack began. The Red Sticks were held off and suffered a loss of many, but regrouped.

After keeping the town of Tuckabatchee under siege for seven days, the Red Sticks and prophets decided on the eight day, which would have been July 22nd, "the town was to be sunk," and plans for a large scale attack were made. According to Joel W. Martin, in his book, Sacred Revolt, this timing was of symbolic significance. The number eight was a multiple of the number four, which stood for the cardinal directions and creation. To the Creeks, this was sacred. This may have been their reasoning, and I think the timing was right to attack, but apparently the big attack never happened.

At an opportune time during the dark of night, a brave warrior slipped out of Tuckabatchee and reached Cusseta, obtaining help for the besieged town. More than two-hundred Cusseta and Coweta Warriors arrived at Tuckabatchee and broke the siege, escorting Big Warrior and the others back to Coweta. With their own ammunition low and having received loss of men, the Red Sticks offered no resistance. Taking with them only what could be carried on their backs, the group of friendly Tuckabatchee Creeks was allowed to go. The Red Sticks took the last action. If any of the retreating group looked back, they would have seen smoke from Tuckabatchee filling the summer sky.

The Lower Creek town of Coweta now became the headquarters of the friendly Creeks, where hundreds had gathered. Included in the number were the five-hundred warriors from white towns and the Cherokee who had finally sent two-hundred men. The chiefs had asked for help from Hawkins and the Governor of Georgia, but Hawkins only sent food and supplies, unwilling at that time to become involved in the Creek Civil War. So, it was agreed that in mid August the seven-hundred would go in search of about twenty-five hundred Red Stick Warriors.

This must have been horrifying for the friendly warriors. Modern movies and books portray the Creeks and all Indians for that matter, as blood thirsty heathens ready, without any hesitation or remorse, to brutally kill their victims. This statement from the book, The Southern Indians and Benjamin Hawkins, by Florette Henri, may surprise the reader, but "the Creeks as a people did not enjoy killing of any kind, and obviously they could have no stomach at all for killing the youth of their nation."

The undermanned war parties still searched, I imagine, hoping not to find the elusive Red Sticks. I do not know if the brave warriors from Coweta found their foe at that particular time or not, but the red town of Talisi was destroyed, most likely in retaliation for the siege and destruction of Tuckabatchee. As I mentioned previously, Talisi was a hot bed for the prophets and Red Stick leaders, including Peter McQueen and Hopohielthle Micco. The prophet's headquarters then moved down river a few miles to the town of Autossee, which was located on the left bank of the river near the mouth of Caleebee Creek.

Such was the story, the true story I might add, of the siege of Tuckabatcheee and the destruction of both of our towns. I find this fascinating and wish that I could discover more information about Talisi and Tuckabatchee's participation in the Creek Civil War. Maybe, I should reveal now which side I would have been on had I lived two-hundred years ago, the Red Stick side or the White Peace side? I do not hesitate at all when I say that I would have been on the losing side … but wait, both sides lost, did they not? Let us move on now to documented information regarding our towns.

Chapter 28
Burnt Corn

Unlike the construction of buildings and homes in modern times, which can take months or even years, the rebuilding of the towns of Talisi and Tuckabatchee was quite simple and quick. In this time period, all structures were of timber from felled trees, so the material was available to rebuild. The greatest loss would have been personal objects and the food supply. The town of Tuckabatchee, which was an extremely large town, probably was not entirely destroyed, but seventeen-hundred bushels of corn stored there was surely confiscated by the Red Sticks. Planting corn and other crops had not been a top priority for them the previous spring, and the Red Sticks and their families would suffer greatly from lack of food during the future months of the war.

Tensions continued to increase between the Red Stick faction and the peace groups. At this point, the Red Sticks did not intend to go to war with the whites, but at the same time, depredations of their land would not be tolerated. In fact, the area around Tuckabatchee and most of the Creek Nation was not a safe or happy place to be. With guns and ammunition in short supply, it was obvious to the Red Stick leaders that help in securing these items would be necessary. By this time, a large group of hostiles had gathered at the Holy Ground, located on the Alabama River. Some of these warriors, under the command of Peter McQueen from Talisi and Jim Boy, the war chief from Autossee, along with Josiah Francis of the Alibamos, planned a trip to Pensacola in search of the needed war supplies. Some historians say that as many as 350 warriors made the trip, while others say that number was greatly exaggerated. At any rate, when that many excited, hot-headed warriors came together, trouble couldn't be far away. Albert Pickett states in his book, *History of Alabama*, "On their way, they beat and drove off every Indian that would not take the war-talk."

When they arrived at Burnt Corn Spring, which was at that time at the crossing of the Federal and Pensacola Roads and today is located in eastern Monroe County, costly mischief began. Mischief is not really a strong enough word to describe the actions of the Red Stick warriors. Foolish is a better word and surely no thought whatsoever of the consequences was considered before the home of a Mr. Cornells was burned. His wife, along with man named Marlow who lived with them was taken as prisoners to Pensacola. As one can imagine, Mr. Cornells was outraged and frightened for the safety of his wife. It wasn't long for news of the event to spread over the southern frontier, generating much concern and fear. By 1813, a great portion of the Tombigbee/Tensaw area was settled by whites and mestizos, who were, as previously mentioned a White-Creek mixture. Several forts had been constructed which in the coming weeks and months would be used as supposed "safe places."

The Red Stick group continued on their journey to Pensacola. I have no further documentation on whether or not they engaged in further mischief, but I would guess they did. Upon arrival in the Spanish controlled town, the unfortunate Mrs. Cornells was sold for a blanket. The Creek leaders then called on the Governor, presenting him with a letter from a British general. Thinking the letter would authorize the desired ammunition since the British and Spanish were allied against the Americans, the Creeks were disappointed when they received only a time for another meeting. After more negotiations, three hundred pounds of powder and lead was issued. Stating the amount was not enough to meet their needs McQueen then gave the governor a list of all the Creek towns with four-thousand warriors, ready to take the red stick of war. Refusal to provide more ammunition prompted the Creek war leader to declare war on the white Americans. So it seems that Peter McQueen of

Talisi may have voiced the words the southern frontier had feared and dreaded. The Creeks were now at war with the Whites and a war dance was performed in Pensacola.

This information was gathered by a couple of spies, one of which was David Tate, who had Talisi ties as well. On the twenty-fourth of July, 1813 part of the hostile group left Pensacola and the remainder stayed, the reason being unclear. The spies lost very little time in spreading this information and a militia made up of white men, half breeds and friendly Creeks was formed and called out.

On the twenty-seventh of July, the Red Stick Creeks were encamped near Burnt Corn Creek. As the time was near the noon hour, they were preparing and eating their meal, having no idea the militia was on their trail. This seems strange and careless that lookout scouts had not been posted, but apparently they were not, as the Creeks were completely surprised by several hundred militia. The troops opened fire on the warriors as they were sitting or reclining on the ground. Recovering quickly from the surprise attack, the outnumbered Creeks returned fire for a short period of time, but soon gave way in retreat into the swamp. As was the custom of Creeks and other Indians as well, they did rally, running out of the swamp, brandishing their guns and war clubs with cries of vengeance.

While some of the militia had been engaged in the fight, other units had been busy catching and leading off the pack horses, the packs, of course, being filled with the much needed powder and lead. When the Red Stick warriors mounted their rally, the militia had been divided, which allowed the tables to turn. This time the troops of militia panicked and fell back in fear and confusion. The officers did make another stand with a small group of men as McQueen's warriors continued their fire.

The fighting continued for another hour of so, and the Americans began to feel a sense of defeat. Two-thirds of the militia group was in retreat in fact, according to Halbert and Hall from the book, *The Creek War of 1813 and 1814*, which states, "It was a disgraceful rout."

The Red Sticks followed the militia for a mile or so, but were unable to overtake them, which was a good thing, as the chase would have ended in a slaughter of the whites. Which side claimed victory in the Battle of Burnt Corn Creek, the first official battle in the Creek Civil War? The white militia group did retreat with a loss of two men and fifteen wounded. The key word here is retreat and the men involved in the battle received ridicule for many years for their lack of prowess. On the other hand, the Creek warriors lost as many as a dozen, with several more injured, and remember the horses and the packs filled with ammunition were taken in the retreat. So, it would appear that the white led militia had scored first on Talisi's Peter McQueen and his Red Stick warriors, but then there was Fort Mims....

Chapter 29
The Fort

Due to lack of documentation regarding the Talisi connection with Fort Mims, I do not intend to spend much time on the subject, but some facts need to be mentioned.

That particular area, near the confluence of the Tombigbee and the Alabama Rivers which includes the current counties of Washington, Clark and Monroe, had been settled by whites for several years. In fact, Washington was the first to become a county being founded in 1800, while the area was still a part of the Mississippi Territory. Many of the Creek families, having been influenced by the white settlers and through the intermarriage of the two races, had quickly adapted to white culture. Also, some of the Creeks, William Weatherford for example, had obtained wealth and had plantations in the area. So, this was not the typical Creek community. As white settlers had moved into this region, stockades or little forts had been built for protection from the "other" Creeks, sometimes referred to as the savages. The unrest increased during the period prior to the Creek Civil War and more stockades were constructed. Fort Mims was one such stockade. Shortly after the Burnt Corn incident, area families, including Creeks and mixed bloods converged at the home of Indian countryman Samuel Mims. The home, located about a mile from the Alabama River, was quickly made into what was considered to be a secure safe place. We know that on Monday, August 30, 1813, the stockade was anything but secure and what ensued was later to be called the Fort Mims Massacre.

The news spread across the countryside that white families, including women and children, had been heinously murdered by the savage Red Sticks. The incident was terrible and never should have happened and possibly would not have if not for inattentive factors. The number of people at Fort Mims and their racial makeup vary from historian to historian. The information I have from Halbert and Ball, gives a total number of 553 with 265 or so being soldiers. Some were white, some Spaniards, some colored, but most were of mixed Indian blood. My research indicates that most of the whites had some kind of Creek connection. This, unlike the newspapers of the time implied, was not an attack solely on the white people, but on the Creeks who chose to live like the whites.

One of the inattentive factors mentioned, which could have prevented the atrocity, was the lack of guards. The commanders of the Fort, Captain Dixon Bailey, a half-breed himself, and Major Daniel Beasley, had received word that the Red Sticks were coming their way. For some unknown reason, both men refused to listen and would not acknowledge the impending danger. When Red Stick warriors were sighted by Negroes working in a nearby field, they were told the painted warriors must have been cows. The Negroes were flogged for spreading alarm. A strange reaction from commanders who knew hostiles were in the area.

It was around noon when the Red Sticks came within sight of Fort Mims and they were surprised at what they found. The gate was wide open and the occupants could be seen leisurely eating their meals and enjoying the summer day. When it became apparent that the painted warriors brandishing their war clubs and filling the air with their war whoops had not come for a friendly visit, it was too late. The danger then being realized, the soldiers attempted to close the gate. Another factor, the gate would not close. The summer rain and wind or possibly constant traffic through the entrance, had formed piles of sand against the gate. The Red Stick warriors had not expected the "door" to be open for them.

I believe the original intent was not the slaughter that transpired, but to frighten and warn of possible future attacks. Nonetheless, according to one source, the Red Sticks led by Red Eagle and Talisi's Peter McQueen as well as other Tallapoosa River area warriors, stormed the fort. I think the Red Sticks were high on excited momentum and after finding the gate open and facing no organized opposition to their entry, things got sadly out of hand.

The results, regardless of reason or race of the victims were horrible with around five-hundred being brutally killed. This number varies, mainly due to conflicting numbers of original occupants of the fort. Remember too, that nearly half those inside were soldiers and that many of the Red Sticks were killed in the attack as well. This would add to the total number of deaths accounted for in the battle.

It was over. The event had happened. Nothing would change, even if the Red Stick warriors had wanted it to. This was a day that would go down in Alabama history as a black mark on the Creek people. Helpless women and children had been needlessly killed. This, the white people said, had been a massacre, the Fort Mims Massacre. It was wrong and no matter how hard I try to rationalize and make it right, I cannot. I still think if proper defensive action had been used, if the threat of danger had been taken seriously, if the gate had been closed and guards had been posted, if there had been any organized resistance at all, the Red Stick warriors attack would have not been as deadly.

This, as I said earlier, had not necessarily been an attack just on whites, but on their own race, their own people, who in the eyes of the Red Stick faction had turned away from the old ways and the Creek culture.

After Fort Mims, the minor incidents that had occurred on the southern frontier suddenly became a national threat. These outrages on the white settlers would not be tolerated and the savage Indians would be punished to whatever degree was necessary. How dare they attack the white settlers on their own land? Wait, I think something is wrong here;

the land belonged to the Creeks. Unfortunately, the event at Fort Mims was the official beginning of the loss of that land. Troops from Mississippi, Georgia and Tennessee converged on the territory over the next few months and the Red Stick force and their people suffered.

My few little facts which needed to be mentioned turned into many, but I think it necessary that the events of Fort Mims be known. Also, that Peter McQueen and others from Talisi had been participants in some form or other in the incident which turned the tide for the Creek people.

* * * * * * * *

It is still there, after two-hundred years, an intense feeling of tragic sadness fills the space that was Fort Mims. I experienced that sensation immediately in May of 2003, when Randall and I visited the remains of the old fort site. Located a few miles away from the community of Stockton, near the Boatyard, a backwater lake of the Alabama River, the fort and the surrounding area seems entrenched in infinite history.

The sparsely populated region with practically every tree hung heavy with gray Spanish moss and the smell of the river can transport one to another time. It certainly did for me as we stepped from the present back into the past.

I was surprised at the small size of the fort which is outlined with only creosote posts. It seems amazing that so many people could have been enclosed inside of the space. We walked from each interpretive plaque, each explaining what had happened at every particular point within the fort. The open gate entrance, the site of the Mims house and the overall tragedy which occurred on that hot August day, filled me with an overwhelming desire to look over my shoulder, expecting to see the painted Red Stick Warriors brandishing their war clubs, rushing into the fort. Part of me wanted to leave quickly, but then I also wanted to stay to experience the feeling that was forever locked in time.

I would recommend a visit to Fort Mims. Maybe you too can feel that moment in time.

Chapter 30
Autossee

Fear now was the prevailing emotion in the Creek frontier. The white and mixed-breed families nervously awaited the next attack from the painted warriors. The warriors knew that retaliation was inevitable and they, while not afraid for themselves, did fear for their families. Many of the women and children were taken south to stay with other family members and friends in Florida. This was wise, as a full scale effort to subdue the Red Stick movement was underway. While there were several attacks on stockades and farms, mainly in the lower Alabama River area, none compared to Mims. The next event with Talisi connections which was termed as a battle was the Battle of Autossee. Before I get to the battle, I need to expand about this town, as I have not done so before.

Autossee-Atassi, two of several ways to spell the town and meaning war club, was an ancient town. Autossee was not mentioned in *The DeSoto Chronicles*, but was included in the Luna Narratives in 1560, as Atachi and was listed on later maps of 1675 and 1725 as Atassi, surely, the same town. As with many Creek towns, Autossee moved from one location to another, one site below the falls above Tuckabatchee, another five miles below Calebee Creek. Neither of these locations has been identified as positive sites for Autossee. The third site, about five miles down river from Tuckabatchee at the mouth of Calebee Creek is the site agreed on by historians and archaeologist as Autossee. I have never actually been on the site, but I have stood across the river and viewed the area. If one did not know, it would look like a dozen other places on the river where a creek enters the Tallapoosa. To me it is a special place. I could easily visualize the Creek people going about their daily activities and also the bloody battle which occurred there.

One of the Autossee sites — and I am pretty sure, the one mentioned above — was described by a visitor in the 1770s as being quite fantastic, the houses being decorated with paintings and sculptures of animals and serpents. The use of huge longleaf pine logs, which had been transported from other areas, added a look to Autossee not normally seen in the Tallapoosa River Valley, making the town unique and mysterious. By the early 1800s, having lost its grandeur, Autossee had become a small, poverty stricken town. The town must have regained some of its former population and appearance by 1813.

And now we move on to the battle. During the Creek Civil War, Autossee became a Red Stick Mecca, with as many as 2,000 warriors converging on the town. Red Stick war leader Peter McQueen, other leaders and prophets were included in the number of hostiles. In late November 1813, General John Floyd, and his 950 Georgia militia, along with 450 friendly Creeks, made their way toward the Tallapoosa River and the war town of Autossee. The friendly Creeks included groups from Coweta, under the leadership of William McIntosh, who distinguished himself during the battle, and Autossee's up-river neighbors from Tuckabatchee, led by Chief Mad Dog's son, who fought with bravery, but was killed.

According to one source, the Red Sticks were surprised and yet another claims they were expecting an attack and were prepared. I think they knew the militia was coming, how could they not know? They would have had scouts and guards patrolling the area. I do think though, the surprise was when the attack came.

Daybreak on the 29th day of November was calm, clear and very cold. The fields surrounding Autossee were white with frost. I imagine the warriors were still in the warmth of their houses when the attack first began. According to Stiggins, in his Creek Indian History, immediate orders were given to take the old men, the women, children and Negroes to a down-river place of safety at the nearby town of Clewalla. Floyd and his men planned to surround the town, but may have been a little surprised in finding not one but two towns, the second being about 500 yards below the first on the opposite side of Calebee Creek. This must have been where the women and children were positioned, how else could they have escaped?

Three companies of infantry along with mounted troops began the attack. This was the first time ever that soldiers, other than the red warrior, invaded the banks of the Tallapoosa. Also, for the first time, the thundering sound of the cannon filled the otherwise peaceful and tranquil valley. The Red Sticks advanced, but were soon driven back into the thickets. The prophets rallied the warriors, encouraging them to fight with total abandon. Although the Red Sticks may have outnumbered Floyd's troops, they were greatly overmatched by military weaponry. The friendly Creeks were then ordered to cross the river to cut off any attempt at escape. The Tallapoosa River in November is cold, very cold and at the point of confluence of Calebee Creek, the depth would require swimming. The difficulty the friendly Creeks had in crossing the river, allowed time for the Red Sticks to hide in caves in the bluff overlooking the river. There are many high bluffs along the river, and I have heard caves mentioned, but I'm not sure the terrain is suitable for one of any size. Possibly, the Red Sticks had cut the caves in the bluffs for occasions like this one, or maybe they were actually ravines or ditches. A ravine in past generations may have been called a cave. Many of the Red Sticks attempted to hide in the thick underbrush, but were found and killed by Floyd's troops. Lasting for three hours, fire was heavy from both sides and many were wounded and killed.

Floyd amazingly enough, only lost a dozen men, while the Red Stick warriors suffered a severe blow. Two hundred warriors, including chiefs and prophets would not live to fight another day. According to Creek custom, their dead were never left behind and slain red warriors were dragged down the bluff to the river. On a cold day in November 1813, the Tallapoosa River ran crimson with the blood of its warriors.

After the battle, incriminating evidence, including white scalps and other personal items were discovered indicating to Floyd that the perpetrators of the Fort Mims Massacre had been defeated. Not being satisfied to merely defeat the Red Sticks on their own ground, Floyd fired several cannon rounds, destroying the houses of the hapless Autossee. One source states that four-hundred buildings were destroyed, including those with the ornate architecture filled with valuable native articles.

Maybe one day I will be able to go to the site and visualize what had been all those years ago. Unfortunately, the site is very near a gravel pit and is owned by a sand and gravel company. Hopefully, the owners will realize the historical significance and the site of Autosse will not be hauled off truck load by truck load.

In the battle's aftermath, Floyd gathered up his wounded and dead and formed a line of march and left the smoldering town. The friendly Creeks did not follow him, but stayed to pillage and take what was left from the houses of their neighbors.

About a mile east of the battle site, the militia stopped to bury their dead. Near the site, once called Heydon's Hill, but now lost in time, the Red Sticks attacked the rear guard. Only a few shots were fired and the warriors retreated while Floyd and his Georgia militia continued back to Fort Mitchell. The route taken was not given, but I imagine the Federal Road was used by the victorious group.

While on this campaign, the towns of Little Talisi, which was located near Wetumpka, and also our Talisi were burned yet again. Remember, Talisi was destroyed by the Tuckabatchee in retaliation in July of that same year. I have not been able to find more than just the slightest mention of the destruction of the towns by Floyd. Apparently, no battle occurred and the towns were simply torched. I do wonder about the distance between Autossee and Little Talisi. Movement by an army the size of Floyd's would surely have been noted in the historical record, and if he left Autossee for Fort Mitchell after the battle, then he must have burned Little Talisi, located on the Coosa River first. That does not add up to me. It would not have been any problem for Floyd's troops to have gone up river to burn our Talisi, but why is there not more information about that? So, I think I will have to leave it at that, but I do wonder if maybe some writer along the way may have gotten facts confused. Being perfectly honest, many facts may have been confused or embellished, but that, after all, is how history is often told. We take what we have.

We do know the battle of Autossee did, in fact, happen, and many, too many Red Stick warriors were lost. They would regroup, refusing to give up the fight for their homeland and those who were left would fight again.

Chapter 31
Unholy Ground

Attacks and skirmishes between the Red Sticks and the encroaching whites and their allies continued including a major one at the Holy Ground. The Holy Ground site was located on the Alabama River in Lowndes County near present day White Hall. This was a town where principal prophets lived and others gathered. As the Creek War intensified, the Holy Ground supposedly became a sacred place where whites could not tread. General F.L. Claiborne, along with his Mississippi Militia and some friendly Choctaw had no problem disproving this belief. I am not going into any great length with the story of the battle of the "Holy Ground" since there is little if any information regarding Talisi connections.

The battle did occur on December 23, 1813, and as with the Battle of Autossee, the victory belonged to the white intruders. Thirty-three Creeks were killed, of that number twenty-one were actually Indians and twelve were Negroes. This was the first time that Creek slaves — yes they did have slaves — fought along side their masters in the Alabama frontier. One of the leading Creek prophets as well as a Shawnee prophet was killed. Neither prophet's name is known.

The primary reason that I include the Holy Ground battle in my story is due to the legendary actions of William Weatherford, the Red Eagle. When the prophets and warriors realized that Holy Ground was actually not any different from any other place and was not holy after all, they proceeded to retreat into the cane breaks, while others crossed the river.

The Red Eagle was the only warrior remaining and finding himself in extreme danger, made a decision of escape of which legends are made. The village site of Holy Ground was built on a high bluff over looking the river. Some embellished versions have Red Eagle upon his fabulous horse Arrow, leaping thirty or forty feet into the Alabama.

Yet another version from Thomas Woodward, conflicts that entirely, stating that Red Eagle led his horse down a ravine, then into the river, without jumping at all. No one really knows for sure, but I think the most logical version comes from Halbert and Ball. The fleeing warrior with a running start jumped about twelve feet down, extending twenty feet out into the swift Alabama River. With musket balls sailing all around, Red Eagle and Arrow safely crossed the river. One shot did cut off a lock of hair from the horse's mane. Obviously, the Great Spirit had plans for Red Eagle to fight for his people yet again.

I relay this fascinating part of the battle to point out an erroneous Talisi connection. In one history of Tallassee, which was written many years ago, the writer leads one to believe that Red Eagle made his leap from a rock bluff on Lake Tallassee. This rock bluff, known as Red Nose Rock, is located on the west side of the river, a little over a mile north of the Benjamin Fitzpatrick Bridge.

Before the rock formations were dynamited during the construction of Thurlow Dam, the rock did resemble the face of a man. Mineral deposits may have given a red tint to the rock, but Red Eagle's legendary leap did not occur here. I guess it made for a good story, but it was just that.

Chapter 32
Calebee

The next battle with a Talisi connection was the Battle of Calebee Creek. In late January 1814, Floyd and the Georgia militia again moved into the Calebee Creek Valley. This time General Floyd had seventeen-hundred men under his command, along with four to six-hundred friendly Indians. He undoubtedly planned to make sure he had enough manpower to fight the force of Red Sticks, which may have numbered thirteen-hundred.

Needless to say, the Red Stick warriors had few guns and even less ammunition. By this point in the Creek War they had resorted to the use of weapons of old — bows, arrows and hatchets — no match for the guns and cannons they would face. Knowing the location of the white army, the Red Sticks planned their attack. The Red Eagle was there, but did not agree with the battle plans and left the night beforehand.

Before the first rays of sun would brighten the sky on the morning of January 27, 1814, the Red Stick warriors, including Peter McQueen, readied for the attack. Floyd and his entourage were camped on the banks of the Calebee Creek, seven miles west of the current town of Tuskegee. This would put the site about half way between that town and Talisi. I have never been to the site, but I think from my research, the location was between the Calebee Creek Bridge on U.S. Highway 80 and the Tallapoosa River.

The Red Sticks hid in the undergrowth along the creek and initiated the attack at daylight. But, as in previous battles, superior manpower and weaponry led to yet another victory for the white militia. This battle brought to an end the campaigns of General Floyd and other military forces in the area. After losing even more warriors in the Battle of Calebee Creek, the unity of the Red Sticks began to waver. This was the final battle to be fought in the lower Tallapoosa River Valley.

Chapter 33
The Horseshoe

Moving up river to the site known as Tohopeka, several Red Stick towns had gathered for one final stand and there was a Talisi connection. The upper Tallapoosa towns of Oakfuskee, New Youka, Oakchay, Hillibee and Fish Pond, were undoubtedly joined by warriors from Talisi and Autossee.

In early spring of 1814, a veteran soldier led his troops of Tennessee Militia deep into Creek territory. His goal was to quell the uprising of the hostiles. Called Old Hickory by his men, and Sharp Knife by the Creek, General Andrew Jackson had no love for the Indians and would use the events of the day to help vault himself into the presidency of the United States.

The date was Sunday, the 27th of March 1814; history has it as being a cool, sunny day. The warriors of the combined towns, anticipating Jackson, had made preparations, constructing a vast barricade, extending across the peninsula, which was encircled by the winding Tallapoosa. This structure was of heavy construction and the Red Sticks thought it would provide the needed protection. There were one-thousand Red Stick warriors ready to fight and nearly three-hundred women and children in the village to the rear of the barricade near the river.

The scouts knew of his arrival. Jackson lead two-thousand infantry, seven-hundred cavalry and mounted riflemen, and oh yes, the friendly Indians, including five-hundred Cherokee and one-hundred Creek. Among the group of Creeks were some Tuckabatchee, still seeking revenge on their neighbors from Talisi and Autossee.

At 10 o'clock that morning, Andrew Jackson topped the hill overlooking the peninsula. He was impressed, but not concerned, at what he saw. He knew the victory would be his and thought that the Creeks "had penned themselves up for slaughter." Jackson had, in addition to his well armed militia, two cannons, which were placed on the hilltop facing the barricade. By 10:30, he began firing on the poorly armed Red Sticks. They had very few guns now and even the strongest archer had difficulty reaching a target. When Jackson's fire began, the sound of war drums and yells of defiance from the hostiles and prophets filled the brisk air. This continued for about two hours, most likely with little harm being done to the barricade, nor the warriors inside. The Red Sticks may have known they would not be able to hold the line of defense and would need a plan of escape. Here lies their costly mistake.

Apparently, if their defense broke, they planned to move the approximate three-quarters of a mile from the barricade to the river and escape. Several canoes had been left carelessly on the river bank. The Red warriors had no idea that Jackson had commanded General John Coffee and his cavalry of seven-hundred, the five-hundred Cherokee and one-hundred friendly Creek to cross the Tallapoosa and block that escape. Without any formal order from anyone, some of the Creek and Cherokee swam the frigid river, taking possession of the canoes and took them back to the waiting cavalry, who then crossed over to the other side.

One has to wonder if any of those Creek were from Tuckabatchee, maybe even being acquainted with some of the Red Sticks. We will never know, but we do know this was the event that set the slaughter in motion. With the village under attack from the rear, this gave Jackson the opportunity he needed to make a frontal assault. What ensued for the next several hours was more horrific than I have words to describe. The Red Sticks gave their all and fought bravely to the end, refusing to surrender. The village, of course, was burned, some accounts say the women and children were taken captive and given to the friendly Creek and Cherokee. Many may have also been killed in the slaughter. I can not understand why the women were not armed and posted as guards.

Perhaps this was the case, but was unsuccessful.

The Red Stick dead on the battlefield was 557 and 300 more died trying to cross the Tallapoosa, again making the river run red. Many others were wounded and probably died later. Twenty-six American soldiers died, with 107 being injured. Had this been an attack on white settlers, history would have labeled it a massacre, but instead was simply called a battle, The Battle of Horseshoe Bend.

I have been to the battle site many times, standing on the bank of the swiftly flowing river where the crossing was made, moving beyond the village area to the place where the barricade stood, the spot where the gallant Red Stick warriors made their last stand. In my mind I could see the warriors, hear their cries and understand what they were fighting for…what every American — and they were truly Americans — have fought for, the freedom to have their land and their home and to live their life. There is a narrated model of the battle inside the on-site museum that says, "At the battle's end the sun was setting and it was setting on the great and proud Creek Nation."

And on that day, it did.

Chapter 34
After the Horseshoe

What happened after the massacre at the Horseshoe? Very little information was written about the time immediately after and I can only speculate. The Red Stick warriors that made their homes on the upper Tallapoosa River were virtually wiped out, with only two-hundred or so remaining. Many of those were wounded and may not have lived. What about their families, the women and children whose homes were destroyed by Jackson and who were taken captive? How were they treated? One source states they were given to McIntosh who took them to Big Warrior at Coweta where some were adopted and others were treated as slaves. Regardless of what happened, their lives were forever changed.

The Red Sticks had suffered defeat before but never such annihilation. This must have left the ones remaining feeling totally helpless, with a tremendous burden of loss and sense of defeat. We do know the few remaining did regroup and returned to their homes along the Tallapoosa, that is, what little was left of their homes. Many of them, including Peter McQueen, gathered their families and fled to Pensacola, hoping to find refuge with other family members who had earlier settled among the Spanish.

I must relate now, what became of that brave, gallant warrior who had called Talisi his home. After an attempt was made by Andrew Jackson and William McIntosh to capture and hang McQueen in Spanish Florida in 1818, he fled across the peninsula and died in lonely exile. This was a sad and not very proud way for one such as Peter McQueen to meet his demise. He was certainly one of Talisi's famous, or some might say, infamous sons.

Then there were those who had no home. The American military searched the countryside for Red Stick villages and burned them. Most of the villages on the upper Tallapoosa River were Red. Left were the ones who were forced to wonder from place to place with no food, except that which nature provided. In March, nature provided very little. This was certainly a sad time for the Creeks, but they were strong people and would survive this and much more, for awhile anyway.

The British tried to rally the Red Sticks again by promising ammunition and support, but General Jackson would soon thwart this plan, as usual. Jackson set up camp in April, at the site of Old Fort Toulouse at the junction of the Tallapoosa and Coosa Rivers. The fort was rebuilt and renamed Fort Jackson in honor of the man who had saved the white settlers from the horrible Red Sticks. He actually renamed the fort himself.

Although William Weatherford, The Red Eagle, was not present at the Horseshoe, having left a couple of days prior, Jackson very much wanted his surrender. A point that has not been made clear before should be done so now. Most people think that Red Eagle was the mastermind of the Creek War and the leader of the Red Stick movement. He was neither. Before the uprising, he was William Weatherford, a wealthy plantation owner, living in the Tensaw area of the Mississippi Territory. He just happened to be one-eight Creek and spent much time among his mother's people. When the Red Stick movement began, he did sympathize with the Creeks, knowing they were being treated unfairly. The Red Stick leaders asked for his support and aid. His refusal prompted threats toward his family. When Weatherford refused yet again, according to some sources, his family members were taken hostage. He knew a war with the white race could not be won, they were too many, but having no choice, he became Red Eagle.

He was a brave warrior and a good, intelligent leader and would, of course, become, possibly, the most well known of all Red Sticks. He gained this notoriety even though he was present at only two of all the battles, Fort Mims, where he actually tried to prevent the actions of the

Red Sticks, and at Holy Ground. He would have been at Calebee Creek, but after having a disagreement with other leaders, left before the battle began. I do not know if Jackson knew this about Red Eagle, or like others, assumed him to be the decision maker of the past two years.

Jackson sent messages to all the friendly chiefs, urging them to turn Red Eagle in or force him to surrender, if they wanted peace. He also made it clear that no food supplies would be made available to the women and children until he had Red Eagle in his custody. In my opinion, and I certainly can give one, Andrew Jackson was a despicable person, having no regard for the lives of the Creek people, not even the children. His only concern was to defeat that race of people and to do whatever it took to improve his status.

Learning of the demands of Jackson, Red Eagle, being truly brave, and putting the lives of his people, and they were his chosen people, ahead of his own safety, made the decision to surrender. The soldiers did not recognize him when he entered the camp and he was allowed to walk directly to the tent of Andrew Jackson. Here is the Talisi connection.

Big Warrior was sitting outside Jackson's tent. He was, remember, one of the "friendly" chiefs. From the book *Andrew Jackson and His Indian Wars*, Robert V. Remini quoted Big Warrior in saying, "Ah, Bill Weatherford, have we got you at last?" And Red Eagle's reply, "you_____traitor, if you give me any insolence I will blow a ball through your cowardly heart." Hearing the exchange, Jackson came outside the tent and was surely surprised to see Red Eagle in person, standing in front of him. "How dare you, sir, to ride up to my tent after having murdered the women and children at Fort Mims." Red Eagle defiantly answered, "General Jackson, I am not afraid of you. I fear no man, for I am a Creek warrior." Realizing that the guns of several soldiers were pointed at him, ready to fire with just a word from their commander, he continued, "I am in your power, do with me what you please. I am a soldier still. I have done the white people all the harm I could. I have fought them, and fought them bravely. If I had an army, I would fight them still. But I have none! My people are no more! Nothing is left me but to weep over the misfortunes of my country."

Many in the camp clamored for his death right then and there, but Jackson recognizing the bravery and compassion of this warrior, silenced his men. Red Eagle told Jackson he wanted peace and for the suffering of his people to end. He had known from the beginning this was a war that could not be won or even finished by his Creek people. He had no other choice. He could no longer call his warriors to fight, for his warriors lay scattered on the battlefields, never more to answer his call.

Red Eagle asked for protection and assured Jackson he would talk with his people and they would listen. Jackson, who suddenly found great admiration for his former red foe, permitted him to leave and go in search of his people who were scattered in the forest and cane breaks. The warning was issued, "If you choose to try the fate of arms once more, and I take you prisoner, your life shall pay the forfeit of your crimes. But if you really wish for peace, stay where you are and I will protect you."

No other report of exchange of words between Red Eagle and Big Warrior were written, but I imagine there were some. The two men apparently were never friends, one, giving in to white pressure and the other standing up for the rights of the Creek people, but ironic circumstances prevailed in the end, which I will reveal shortly.

For the next several days, just as Red Eagle had promised, the hostile Creeks, who had become refugees, wandered into Fort Jackson. They were given food, the first many had had in days. Although downtrodden over their current situation, the food was gratefully accepted. For their safety, they were then sent to Fort Williams, which was located up the Coosa River.

Chapter 35
The Treaty

In mid April, the United States War Department, satisfied that the Creeks were under control and that Jackson had brought an end to the war, relieved him of command of Fort Jackson, and he was sent back to Tennessee. He returned in August to help negotiate the TREATY.

All of the Creek chiefs, the friendly and the hostile, were ordered to convene at Fort Jackson on August 1, 1814. They were told that failure to obey this order would result in "unconditional submission." Jackson planned for this to be a complete capitulation by all the Creeks, making no exception. The friendly chiefs wondered why their "friend" was using such threatening language toward them and what was this about treaty terms?

On the appointed day all the friendly chiefs appeared; the Red Stick leaders paid no attention to the demand. My research does not indicate if Red Eagle was present or not. The chiefs were expecting to be praised and even given gifts for their loyalty and service during the Creek War. Instead, nothing of the sort happened and they found out just what type of person Andrew Jackson really was.

The chiefs had been in communication with Benjamin Hawkins regarding the treaty, so they were expecting one, but they were dismayed, shocked, angry and very upset when the contents of the treaty were read to them. The friendly chiefs, even those who had fought against their friends and family members, would be treated no different than the hostile Red Sticks. They had been lied to, tricked and deceived and realized now that Sharp Knife Andrew Jackson's purpose had been to break the power of the Creek Confederacy and seize the land.

Big Warrior, being the speaker of the Nation, tried with no success, to reason with Jackson. He told him that the friendly Creeks had not listened to Tecumseh when he came to speak with them at Tuckabatchee. They had not sided with their Red Stick brothers, but instead had fought along side the whites. How could the so-called Great Father in Washington treat them in such a manner? Other chiefs also tried to persuade Jackson to reconsider, but the answer was the same … sign the treaty or you will be considered enemies of the United States and will be treated as such.

The friendly chiefs talked among themselves and the next day again appeared before Jackson. One can only wonder what the reason could possibly be for what Big Warrior would do next. He offered Jackson and Hawkins each a large tract of land — three square miles to be exact — and the location would be of their choice. Big Warrior said this was out of respect and a token of gratitude. Sounds like a bribe, a desperate attempt to salvage what was most dear to the Creek Nation, their homeland. But wait! That may not have been the reason. Some historians think this was actually an act of contempt for Andrew Jackson and all that he stood for. Jackson apparently decided to accept the land, if approved by the president. He said he would sell the land and give the Creeks clothing for their "naked women and children." The chiefs told him they did not give him the land for clothing, but for him to live on and when he died for his family to always know what the Creek Nation had given him. I am not sure if the transaction actually took place, but it certainly would have given Jackson choice land in Creek territory before it was ceded to the United States.

On the ninth day of August 1814, at 2 P.M., in an act of "capitulation," or unconditional surrender, the friendly chiefs of the Creek Nation signed the treaty Sharp Knife Jackson had forced on them. Twenty-three million acres, three-fifths of the present State of Alabama and a portion of Georgia were given over and was more than any other Southeastern tribe had ever surrendered or would surrender until removal. The chiefs were also forced to give their continued loyalty to the United States and were told that they would be expected to pay for the expense of the war.

Jackson was very pleased with his accomplishments. He had his treaty and all the land that went with it. He apparently had no shame for the trickery he had used. His treaty was not with the Red Sticks he had fought, but with the friendly Creeks who had helped him defeat them. The Creek Civil War ended as a huge land grab for the United States and was yet another step toward the end for the great Creek civilization as they knew it.

And now the ironic circumstance that I alluded to earlier. At some point around this time, Red Eagle went to the home of Andrew Jackson, The Hermitage, located in Nashville, Tennessee. Jackson provided him sanctuary for about a year until it was safe for him to return home. He also provided Red Eagle with two horses for his return trip. He would then become William Weatherford, once again, resuming his previous life as a farmer on his plantation, no longer a hostile Red Stick warrior.

Big Warrior, on the other hand, returned home to inform the Creeks of what had transpired. What a pitiful sight. The proud chiefs of the great and formidable Creek Nation were now totally downtrodden and beaten. Some went home, while others were forced to find a new one. Fortunately, the ceded lands did not include the Talisi and Tuckabatchee areas.

Would the fate of Big Warrior been any different if he had followed the path of Red Eagle and Pete McQueen or if he had taken the red stick of war offered by Tecumseh? We will, of course, never know, but the end result would have eventually been the same. Regardless of how things could have been, on that day, Big Warrior and the other friendly chiefs gathered their meager possessions and headed back toward the rising sun. They regrouped and rebuilt, again finding the way to survive yet another day.

People of the Townhouse

Chapter 36
Back Home on the Tallapoosa

It would not be completely accurate to say that life returned to normal after the land session treaty had been signed. Too many warriors had fought to the end, too many had no home and too many were hungry. The tranquil waters of the Tallapoosa did have a soothing effect on her people. They again planted corn and beans and hunted deer for their food. They played their ball games and continued their ceremonial dance that would reunite the Tuckabatchee and Talisi. The Creeks realized their lives had forever changed. The land along the Tallapoosa was still theirs and they were free to come and go as they wished, as long as the boundaries were recognized. To make sure the Creeks remembered things were different, a string of supply forts were constructed throughout their territory in 1814 and 1815. These forts were on or close to the infamous Federal Road and were about twelve miles apart, or what was considered a day's ride on horseback. They were built and manned by American soldiers. It sounds to me like the government wanted to keep watch on the Creeks, to make sure the surviving Red Stick warriors did not cause any more trouble. One of two forts nearest to Tuckabatchee was Fort Decatur, which was built in April of 1814, by Holmer Milton and his South Carolina militia. One of the company commanders would become Big Warrior's son-in-law, Captain William Walker. Walker's descendants still live in the Tallassee area.

Decatur was located a little less than a mile or so down river from the "Big Bend" in the Tallapoosa and across the river from the extreme lower edge of Tuckabatchee. Anyone who has traveled that part of the river by boat knows there are actually two "Big Bends," the first one, of course, where the Eufaubee meets the Tallapoosa and the second three miles below the first. Both bends make wide turns, changing the direction of the river from due south to due west. The flow of the Tallapoosa over hundreds or maybe even thousands of years has created gravel bars that extend several acres in the bends.

* * * * * * * *

My husband and I have been to both locations many times. If there is a more tranquil place in the entire world, then I do not know about it. Sitting on the gravel in the warm sun, watching the river flowing swiftly over the rocks, hearing the cry of a red tail hawk as it circles overhead in the brilliant blue sky, just as if time had stopped and the Tuckabatchee people were there with us … and maybe they were.

* * * * * * * *

Now, here is more information about Fort Decatur. Around the second bend and just a few hundred yards down river and on the left bank, up on a high bluff, sits the remains of old Fort Decatur. This must have been an impressive site in 1814, nestled among the trees, overlooking the Tallapoosa with a grand view of Tuckabatchee off on the north horizon. The structure was of log, square in shape, encircled by redoubt and possibly fortified

The fort was visited by many distinguished people, including the first governor of Tennessee, John Sevier, who died here. In September 1814, Sevier, also a land speculator, was involved in a boundary settlement between the Creek Nation and the State of Georgia. He took sick and passed away on the 24th of the month and was buried at Fort Decatur, but later re-interred in Tennessee.

The Decatur site is located in the Milstead community and the property is owned today by Auburn University, who plans to preserve the site. The earthen redoubt which outlines the fort wall is still very visible and the remains of an iron fence can still be seen. Inside the fence, a historical group placed a plaque showing the burial site of Governor Sevier. Unfortunately, there was very little information written about the fort and as I stated earlier, it was one of many.

Even less is known about a smaller fort that was constructed just across from Fort Decatur on the north side of the river. This was Fort Burroughs and was constructed about the same time as Decatur. Only the serious historian would know of the existence of Fort Burroughs and only a few today know of the location. We visited the site in March of 2012, and were amazed at the good condition of the remaining redoubt which was also constructed by the South Carolina Militia. The militia camped near this fort since there was very little level ground near Fort Decatur. Fort Burroughs was used as a place to hold court in the Mississippi Territory in 1814 and 1815. Though smaller than Fort Decatur, it was obvious that it once bustled with American troops and I am sure the Tuckabatchee people felt their presence.

With that military presence, the traders who continued to ply their wares and the great influx of settlers passing through the area on the Federal Road, the Tuckabatchee and Talisi people continued to have constant contact with the whites. In 1817, the area became a part of the Alabama Territory and in 1819 the State of Alabama was admitted to the Union. By 1820, the towns of Montgomery, Alabama and Columbus, Georgia, which were on opposite borders of the Creek territory, had become bustling frontier towns. The growth of these white settlements continued to create more contact and had great influence on the Creeks.

The Methodist and Baptist missionaries saw this as a good opportunity to spread the Gospel of Jesus Christ to the unsaved "heathens" (this was the missionary's term). The Creeks knew all about the Great Spirit and Giver of Breath. They knew of a supreme being; they just did not call him God. Some were receptive to the word and the missionaries were allowed to enter the Creek territory.

In the early 1820s, Big Warrior consented to allow both Methodist and Baptist mission schools to be constructed in the Nation. One at Fort Mitchell in present Russell County, and the other called McKendree, located at Tuckabatchee. The fact that the schools did exist is just about all that is known. Along about this time, Reverend Lee Compere and his wife Suzannah established a Baptist mission known as Withington, also in Tuckabatchee. This school was successful and was in operation for three years. Some of the Tuckabatchee opposed the mission and disrupted the school work and teaching. At this point, Big Warrior allowed the teaching to continue, but forbid preaching. The missionaries may have been forcing the Creeks to abandon their religion for that of the whites. Possibly for this reason the school was soon closed. An interesting point regarding Reverend Compere should be noted. He left Tuckabatchee and moved out of the Creek Territory where he would establish the First Baptist Church of Montgomery. There is no documented location for the school, but I think a possible site would be within the upper region of Tuckabatchee behind the GKN facility on Alabama Highway 229. I also believe this area may have been the site of one of the many trading posts that operated in Tuckabatchee. I remember as a child, going to this area and finding, along with the usual array of native artifacts, abundant trade items as well.

Chapter 37
Barent and Millie

Tuckabatchee continued to thrive and remained a very important town in the Creek Confederacy. Many influential men came to the town and, as in the past, many important council meetings were held underneath the branches of the giant oak. Included was the one in May of 1824, when the council passed a law forbidding the sale of any tribal land without the consent of the council, its violation carried the penalty of death. The Tuckabatchee people were accustomed to the white presence in their town; after all they had been around for a long time. One such man became very prominent in the future of Tallassee. (Notice the change in spelling). His name was Barent DuBois.

No early history of our town would be complete without the story of Barent. Being of French ancestry, he was born in New York in 1798. He was actually a fifth generation American. He came to the Tuckabatchee area in the early 1820s as an Indian agent for the American government. The actual meeting and courtship of he and his wife is unknown and any information that might have been recorded is lost in time. Perhaps some day I will write a fictional story about Barent and his bride, but for now I will stick to the facts about Millie, but even those are a little controversial.

She was born in 1809, but where and who her father was is disputed. Some say she was born at Tuckabatchee and her father was Chief Big Warrior. That makes for a good, romanticized story and possibly is true, but on the other hand … genealogy research shows that Millie's father was a trader by the name of Reed, and that she was born on Oakfuskee Creek. Most call this stream Line Creek today and it is, of course, the Macon-Montgomery County line and incidentally was the western boundary of the Creek Nation.

I tend to think the latter is more accurate and I will give my reasons why. Big Warrior did not reside at Tuckabatchee all of the time. He owned and operated a stand — which was the early word for inn — and he also owned a horse racetrack at Warrior Stand, both several miles from Tuckabatchee in present day eastern Macon County.

Big Warrior had a daughter by the name of Millie, but I really do not think she was Barent's Millie. William and Samuel, two of the Dubois' four children, were born on Okfuskee Creek and the other two were born at Tuckabatchee after their parents moved there in 1832. That two of their children were born on Okfuskee Creek and that they moved to Tuckabatchee in 1832 is another good indication that this Millie was not Big Warrior's daughter. Whatever the scenario, Barent and Millie were married in a Creek ceremony.

Barent and Millie moved to the Tuckabatchee area during a very sad and troubling time. Sharp Knife Andrew Jackson became president of the United States in 1828. His plan to remove the Creeks and other southern Indians west of the Mississippi River came into fruition after the Removal Act on March 24, 1832.

During the period after the Creek War of 1813-1814, many of the Creeks living in the area which had not been ceded to the United States may have been lulled into a false security, thinking they would be allowed to keep their land. Yes, the Creeks could keep their land, but only under certain conditions. They would be required to live as the whites and abide by the white man's law or remove to Indian Territory, which is in the modern States of Arkansas and Oklahoma.

Each head of household was entitled to 320 acres and this was doubled for the chiefs and headmen. My question has always been: how could the government give them land that was already theirs? Neither the Creeks nor any other American Indians for that matter had any concept of individual land ownership and how that system worked. To the Creeks, the land was just here. The government was aware of their lack of knowledge and had a plan in place to steal the land almost before it was awarded to them.

White setters had their eye on the Creek land long before the passage of the removal act. Land speculators from the Columbus Land Company and other large towns were sent to Tuckabatchee and Talisi to make deals with the unsuspecting Creeks. These speculators came with the usual array of trade trinkets and the white man's fire water that many Creeks had no will power to resist. These items were either traded for the land or if a large debt had been accumulated by the new landowner, then the lands were taken as payment. Most of the Creeks did not understand what had happened to them and many would lose their land and be forced to leave their homes. Others would accept their allotment and make the best of the situation for awhile until forced removal inevitably took place in a few short years.

Back to Barent and Millie, for their story is not yet finished. They would choose to stay on the Tallapoosa, but obtaining the land due them was difficult. Because they were married in a Creek ceremony, the marriage was not properly recorded. I wonder how many Creek women who married a white man had the same problem. Sounds like another government trick to me.

Since Barent did have ties to the government, he made several trips to Washington, D.C. and the land was finally allotted to them. Barent was a smart man and he was able to obtain much more land. He eventually owned the land on both sides of the river near the falls and he and Millie became wealthy. He was able to make the vision of William Bartram and Benjamin Hawkins come true. Both saw Talisi as a site for a beautiful town.

Barent used the river as a source for power, constructing the first of several mills to be built in Tallassee. Barent was the first white man to live at the present site of Tallassee and became the father of the modern town. He built for his family a fine log house near the site of the present day Community Library and it was still in use as a hospital until torn down in 1939 for the construction of the Fitzpatrick Bridge.

Barent became ill and passed away in July of 1849, at the age of 52. He was buried in the Indian cemetery near the downtown water tank which I mentioned earlier. Later, his body was supposedly re-intered at Rose Hill Cemetery and yet again to the Gauntt Family Cemetery which is located on Gauntt's Mill Road in East Tallassee. One of Barent and Millie's sons married into the Gauntt family, thus the connection, and their ancestors too still reside in the area. There is a headstone located in the Gauntt Cemetery which is a reminder of the legacy left behind for the modern town of Tallassee by Barent DuBois. No one knows for sure which of the three burial sites the final resting place of Barent is.

What became of Millie and the children? According to my research, they continued to live in the home Barent had built for them, hopefully enjoying the prosperity Barent had accumulated. Two of the children, after becoming adults, made the move to Indian Territory. In the spring of 1890, when she was eighty years old, Millie joined them. I can not imagine her being content there; it was too far from her home on the Tallapoosa she had known all of her life. She had been in Indian Territory for only a short time when she became ill. Millie passed away on May 7th and is buried in a cemetery in Oklahoma.

Her body may have been laid to rest there, but I believe her spirit is here with Barent on the banks of the Tallapoosa in the place they called home. And that completes the story of Barent and Millie.

Chapter 38
The Final Sunset

Now we come to the end of the dominant regime of the Creeks in Talisi and Tuckabatchee. After the Removal Act of 1832, the remaining land that once was the Creek Nation was renamed New Alabama. New counties were created, including those of Tallapoosa and Macon. The towns of Talisi and Tuckabatchee were within those two new counties. This again increased friction between the Creek and the thousands of new white settlers who now believed the land was theirs for the taking. This was an extremely turbulent period with sporadic skirmishes between the Creek and Whites.

Gone was most of the Red Stick faction who had pledged to fight to the end. Also gone was Chief Big Warrior, who remained a prominent figure until his death in 1825. He was replaced by other friendly Creeks who wanted only to be left alone, to live and raise their children in peace.

The White settlers and the United States government became impatient and were tired of waiting for the Creeks to remove to Indian Territory on their own. The fertile land in the Tallapoosa River Valley needed to be planted in cotton and the planters demanded the land for their own. I still have trouble understanding this mentality. How can someone take from someone else, just because they want to? That is irrelevant now. The white man wanted the land and he took it.

Sometime in the spring of 1836, the white settlers who had obtained land inside the Creek Nation established the Tallassee Guard. The United States government backed them up by sending troops to force the Creeks at Talisi and Tuckabatchee to pack their belongings and prepare to move. Our local villages held out longer than most, but by fall of 1836, their time was up.

In early September of that year, Tuckabatchee Chief, Opothleyaholo met with General Thomas Jesup of the United States Army. In just over a year, General Jesup became a major factor in a terrible act of treachery. While under a flag of truce, Jesup seized Talisi's Osceloa in the Florida Everglades. The trickery used to capture Osceola eventually led to the death of another one of Talisi's famous sons. Jesup would become the man selected to handle the removal of the Talisi and Tuckabatchee.

Opothleyaholo was the most influential man in the upper Creek Nation, even though he was not the principal chief. He and Jesup were certainly not the best of friends, but they were on good terms, having spent much time together in meetings and council. The General even convinced Opothleyaholo to aid him in calming the resisting Creeks to prevent further uprisings against the whites. Being under pressure from both the United States government and the impatient whites, Jesup urged Opothleyaholo to get his people ready, for they had no choice, they had to go.

Opothleyaholo, who like many of the chiefs who dealt with the government officials, learned how to manipulate and obtain the best deal for his people and also for himself. It was said that he was fond of the white man's fire water and was on some occasions, under its influence. He also may have received special treatment for his cooperation with Jesup. Regardless of this, Opothleyaholo was well liked and trusted by his people and he prepared them for their inevitable journey.

Some call this the Trail of Tears, but I think this phrase was a little more appropriate for the Cherokee who were forced to leave their homes at gunpoint with no time to gather their personal belongings. The Talisi and Tuckabatchee people were at least permitted to do that. Neither did they have delusions of staying here. On the second day of September 1836, under the leadership of Opothleyaholo, more than 2,000 Creeks who had made their home on the banks of the lower Tallapoosa River began their exodus. On September 5th another group of 1,984 departed.

These may have been the first of several groups to leave, as there are accounts on record of some traveling overland while others were placed on boats and sent down river to the gulf and back up the Mississippi to Indian Territory.

There are also names of hundreds of Tuckabatchee and Talisi on a monument located at Fort Mitchell, located in current-day Russell County, indicating departure down the Chattahoochee River from that location.

Not all the Creeks made the trek westward by government force. Some went north to take refuge with their Cherokee neighbors and many others fled to Florida, some staying in the northwestern part of the state while others continued on to the Everglades. Once more these refugees regrouped and fought yet again in the Second Creek War of 1836-1843, which became a part of the Seminole War.

Then there were others who refused to move anywhere. This included those who married into white society, living as they did, as well as the few who hid in the cane breaks and swamps, hoping to avoid the forced removal from their home. Many were actually protected by resident whites and blacks for many years until the fear of removal faded away in the 1880s. Even then, Indian families kept their native blood line a secret into the twentieth century, for fear of being singled out and mistreated for their ancestry.

Imagine this scene; the date is September 2, 1836. The Alabama sky is crystal blue as the sun rises over the east bank of the Tallapoosa, the river that had provided the life-blood for generations of Creeks, the Talisi and Tuckabatchee. They have their possessions bundled together. Some have horses and wagons, but most will begin the trip on foot. There is little conversation among the group; even the children are quiet. There's nothing to say. Some of the women have silent tears steaming down their brown cheeks, but the men, in the tradition of the Creeks, show no emotion.

They are told to begin, facing toward the west, the land known to them as a place of death. What a sad, sad sight this must have been. The fear and uncertainty of not knowing what the future held and the feeling of complete desolation had to have been overwhelming. I imagine they would have stopped just before Tuckabatchee was out of their view, taking one final look at the village that had been their home and the home of their people for thousands of years. Then with one final sigh, the People of the Townhouse would turn and go, never more to see their Tallapoosa home again. They were gone, but they did leave behind something that can never be removed … the Spirit of the Great Muscogee Nation.

I can feel it. Can you?

Epilogue

Today is Tuesday, January 10, 2012, and I have just completed my dream of writing the story about the native people of my town, Tallassee, Alabama. Oh, my goodness! What a thrill to have actually accomplished this goal that I started researching 30 years ago and finally began writing one year ago. I must confess that many times I almost quit writing, thinking it silly to believe I could do this. The desire to write was too strong and I think the Spirit of the Creek may have urged me on as well. Actually, my wonderful husband, Randall, encouraged and inspired me to continue. My purpose was both to educate and entertain in such a manner that anyone from the age of 10 to 80 could easily read and understand the Tallassee Indian story.

I do have one more important point to make that would not fit into the time frame of the book. Over the years, at different times, they did come back. Some came just after removal, refusing to stay in the unfamiliar territory. The blood of these Talisi and Tuckabatchee still courses through the veins of their descendants today in modern Tallassee. Years later, others would come just for a short time, as if searching for something. I remember both my daddy and mother-in-law speaking of the band of "Indians" that came and camped in various places each year. This would have been in the 1930s and 1940s. There have been many accounts since those times of Muscogee visits to the old Tuckabatchee site, and these visits still continue today.

In the summer of 2010, as a part of the Tallassee Homecoming Celebration, a group of Muscogee came from Oklahoma, participating in the celebration program. A very memorable event happened with only a few privileged to see. A traditional ceremony was performed on the rocks in the river near the boat landing behind A.E.S. Industries on

Alabama Highway 229. I will never forget the image of the Muscogee man, dressed as his ancestors, pointing a feather of an eagle in all four directions and then releasing it into the rapidly flowing waters of the Tallapoosa. This was a scene that transcends time, just as it happened centuries ago.

Then, in the fall of 2011, I was fortunate to be involved in the production of the play, *Tecumseh at Tuckabatchee*. This was a fantastic play about Tecumseh's visit to Tuckabatchee in 1811. We were honored to have a Muscogee traditionalist, dancers and dignitaries to visit here with us. They all expressed gratitude for the local interest in the Muscogee heritage.

These modern day Muscogee all came back to the home of their ancestors in search of something. I believe I know what they are searching for, the Spirit of the Great Muscogee, which will rest here eternally on the banks of the Tallapoosa.

Thank you for reading my book.
Debra Taunton Hughey

Bibliography

Cashin, Edward J., *Lachlan McGillivary Indian Trader*
  The Shaping of the Southern Colonial Frontier

Corkran, David, *The Creek Frontier 1540-1783*

Debo, Angie, *The Road to Disappearance*

Ellisor, John T., *The Second Creek War, Interethnic Conflict and Collusion on a Collapsing Frontier*

Funderburk, Emma Lila,
Foreman, Mary Douglas, *Sun Circles and Human Hands*

Griffith, Jr., Benjamin W., *McIntosh and Weatherford, Creek Indian Leaders*

Harris, Stuart W., *Dead Towns of Alabama*

Henri, Florette, *The Southern Indians and Benjamin Hawkins*

Knight, Jr., Vernon James, *Tukabatchee, Archaeological Investigations At An Historic Creek Town, Elmore County, Alabama 1984*

Martin, Joel, *Sacred Revolt*

McReynolds, Edwin C., *The Seminoles*

Pickett, Albert James, *History of Alabama*

Read, William A., *Indian Place Names in Alabama*

Stiggins, George, *Creek Indian History,*
A Historical Narrative of the Genealogy, Traditions And Downfall of the Ispocoga or Creek Indian Tribe of Indians

Southerland, Jr., Henry DeLeon and
Brown, Jerry Elijah, *The Federal Road,*
Through Georgia, the Creek Nation and Alabama 1806-1836

Sugden, John, *Tecumseh, A Life*

Woodward, Thomas, *Woodward's Reminiscences of the Creek or Muscogee Indians*

Wright, Jr., J. Leitch, *Creeks and Seminoles*

Articles

Glenn, Dr. J. M., *Dr. Glenn's Remembrances*

Saxon, Bob, *Indians of Tallapoosa County*

Wadsworth, Dr. Erwin W., *A History of Tallassee*

Additional materials gleaned from hundreds of books on the subject of Native Americans which were read by Debra Hughey over the past 30 years.

Photographical, Art, Map and Sketch Credits

Boraas, Tracey, *American Indian Nations, The Creek Farmers of the Southeast, 1790* portrait of Hopoithle Mico, Talisi Chief and Talisi Chief Opothle Yoholo, a portrait at the time of removal

Catlin, George, National Museum of American Art, Washington, D.C., 1838 Portrait of Osceola

Green, Michael D., *Indians of North America, The Creeks,* map of Talisi and Tuckabatchee

Rothwein, Melessa Taunton, front cover village sketch

Storm, Tripp, Photographer, 2010 Muscogee Ceremony on the Tallapoosa River, by permission of David "Speedy" Harley and Saundra Harley of the Oklahoma Muscogee Nation

Taunton, Dovard, 1984 Painting of Indians spearing stripped bass from the rocks of the Tallapoosa River, by permission of Joe Jeffcoat, owner of artwork

Balance of photographs, personal scenes from Fred Randall and Debra Hughey's collection

www.ingramcontent.com/pod-product-compliance
Lightning Source LLC
Chambersburg PA
CBHW051436290426
44109CB00016B/1573